"A compelling exploration of how comics shape historical memory, Harriet Earle's study of marginalized voices provides an inclusive and nuanced understanding of the Vietnam War's portrayal in American comics. Essential for those interested in the intersection of culture, history, and memory."

—Stephen Connor, associate professor of history at Nipissing University

"Absent speech, scenes concealed in the gutter, the ambiguity of a figure: these are the traces expertly tracked and analyzed in Harriet Earle's exploration of narrative silences within the American mythogenesis of the Vietnam War. This study offers arresting insights for both comics scholars and historians and could offer an interesting counterbalance for teachers who would wish to teach history through comics or other popular media."

—Elizabeth Allyn Woock, assistant professor of English at Palacký University

"This is an important and timely contribution to a neglected but significant part of American comic book history. Although much academic work has concentrated on superhero comics, the war comic has been a hugely popular and important form that has been hugely under-researched. Earle demonstrates that the Vietnam War had an immense impact on the war comic genre.... The complexities of the differing, and continuing, responses to the war in comics are clearly explained in a perceptive and accessible analysis. This is an essential guide for anyone studying the representation of conflict in the comic form."

—David Huxley, editor in chief of *Journal of Graphic Novels and Comics*

SILENCE IN THE QUAGMIRE

 Encapsulations: Critical Comics Studies

SERIES EDITORS
Martin Lund, Malmö University, Sweden
Julia Round, Bournemouth University, United Kingdom

EDITORIAL BOARD
Michelle Ann Abate, The Ohio State University
José Alaniz, University of Washington
Frederick Luis Aldama, The Ohio State University
Julian Chambliss, Michigan State University
Margaret Galvan, University of Florida
A. David Lewis, Massachusetts College of Pharmacy and Health Science
Jean-Matthieu Méon, University of Lorraine, France
Ann Miller, University of Leicester, United Kingdom
Elizabeth Nijdam, University of British Columbia, Canada
Barbara Postema, University of Groningen, Netherlands
Eszter Szép, Independent Researcher, Hungary
Carol Tilley, University of Illinois at Urbana-Champaign

Silence in the Quagmire

The Vietnam War in U.S. Comics

HARRIET E. H. EARLE

UNIVERSITY OF NEBRASKA PRESS   LINCOLN

© 2025 by the Board of Regents of the University of Nebraska

All rights reserved

The University of Nebraska Press is part of a land-grant institution with campuses and programs on the past, present, and future homelands of the Pawnee, Ponca, Otoe-Missouria, Omaha, Dakota, Lakota, Kaw, Cheyenne, and Arapaho Peoples, as well as those of the relocated Ho-Chunk, Sac and Fox, and Iowa Peoples.

♾

Library of Congress Cataloging-in-Publication Data
Names: Earle, Harriet E. H., author.
Title: Silence in the quagmire: the Vietnam War in U.S. comics / Harriet E. H. Earle.
Description: Lincoln: University of Nebraska Press, 2025. | Series: Encapsulations: critical comics studies | Includes bibliographical references and index.
Identifiers: LCCN 2024031916
ISBN 9781496240545 (paperback)
ISBN 9781496242747 (epub)
ISBN 9781496242754 (pdf)
Subjects: LCSH: Vietnam War, 1961–1975—In comics. | Comic books, strips, etc.—United States—History and criticism. | War stories, American—History and criticism. | Psychic trauma in comics. | War in comics. | LCGFT: Comics criticism.
Classification: LCC PN6725 .E23 2025 | DDC 741.5/973—dc23/eng/20240911
LC record available at https://lccn.loc.gov/2024031916

Designed and set in Minion Pro.

Für Carsten, für immer

CONTENTS

List of Illustrations ix

Series Editors' Introduction xi

Acknowledgments xv

Abbreviations xvii

Introduction: The American War 1

1. Visualizing the Vietnamese: Monkeys, Monsters, and the Missing 29

2. From Round-Eye to Sniper Spy: Where Are the Women? 71

3. Broken Kites: Trauma and the Return 102

Conclusion: After the Fall 129

Notes 141

Bibliography 155

Index 169

ILLUSTRATIONS

1. *Jungle War Stories 2* **36**
2. *Super Green Beret 1* **51**
3. & 4. *The 'Nam 7* **58**
5. *The Cape 1969* **67**
6. *The Punisher: Born* **82**
7. *Punisher: The Platoon* **84**

SERIES EDITORS' INTRODUCTION

Martin Lund and Julia Round

U.S. comic books have been persistent and ardent commentators on the nation's wars and other—euphemistically circumscribed[1]—military engagements at least since Superman, Captain Marvel, and many of their superhuman contemporaries started searching high and low for spies and fifth columnists in the years before the attack on Pearl Harbor. From superhero comics to war comics to memoir to reportage, comics creators' approaches to war can range from jingoistic to critical, but rarely are they straightforward or univocal, no matter which war (or "war") we focus our scholarly gaze on.

Many such comics have been written about the Vietnam War, but none have yet been studied extensively. While scholars have explored the ways that comics creators have represented, justified, or criticized U.S. conduct during and after the Second World War, the Korean War, or the War on Terror, for example, there exist few similar studies of Vietnam. By offering the first book-length academic study of Vietnam War–themed comics, Harriet Earle's *Silence in the Quagmire: The Vietnam War in U.S. Comics* thus fills a significant empirical gap in comics scholarship.

This book also takes a different angle than might be expected in its choice of comics for study and in its aim, as it is not intended to be a complete survey of comics produced about this war. Scholarship on war comics has tended to privilege the analysis of combatants or the reproduction of dominant ideologies. Here, Earle focuses instead on less-often-discussed actors—women, veterans, and the Vietnamese—whose presence in these comics is mostly marked by absence, invisibility, or marginality. By centering silenced and marginalized perspectives and voices, this book offers a refreshing approach that promises to benefit further scholarship on comics and armed conflict.

By combining a focus on comics that have only received limited scholarly attention to date with an approach to war comics that brings the margins into the center of attention, Earle's book also speaks to the aims of this series. In the creation of comics or graphic novels, "encapsulation" refers to the artistic and cognitive process whereby panels, images, words, and page layout create meaning and engage the reader. These connotations of selection and design underpin the aims of Encapsulations. Our series of short monographs offers close readings of carefully delineated bodies of comics work with an emphasis on expanding the critical range and depth of comics studies.

By looking at understudied and overlooked texts, artists, and publishers, Encapsulations facilitates a move away from the same "big" and oft-examined texts. Instead, the series uses more diverse case studies to explore new and existing critical theories in tune with an interdisciplinary, intersectional, and global approach to comics scholarship. With an eye toward breaking established patterns and forging new opportunities for scholarship, books in the series advance the theoretical grounding of comics scholarship and broaden critical knowledge of global comics. By showcasing new interdisciplinary perspectives and addressing emerging conceptual, formal, and methodological problems, Encapsulations promotes new approaches, contributes to the diversity of comics scholarship, and delves into uncharted sections of the comics archive.

Compact, affordable, and accessibly written, books in the Encapsulations series are addressed to the interested general reader as well as to scholars and students. These volumes provide teachable, critical texts that foster a deeper general understanding of comics' cultural and historical impact, promote critical public literacy, and expand notions of what's worthy of academic study. We are excited for Harriet Earle's book to join this endeavor and see her analyses of war comics as a welcome invitation for comics studies to follow suit in further centering the marginalized and recognizing silence as a form of discourse that can, and often does, speak volumes—if only we are ready to listen.

ACKNOWLEDGMENTS

No book is created by the author alone; that would surely be impossible. Here, I want to offer my deepest and most heartfelt appreciation to everyone who has helped and supported me in the writing of this book.

First, thank you to Dr. Martin Lund and Dr. Julia Round, Emily Casillas, and the editorial team at the University of Nebraska Press for making this book into a reality. Thank you to the reviewers for their rigor, wisdom, and excellent reports. To Jeremy Hall for his meticulous and elegant copyediting. And to Jess Farr-Cox—another stellar index! Thank you!

Thank you to Sheffield Hallam University for offering research support, with special thanks to Professor Doug Hamilton and Dr. Kaley Kramer. Thank you to Caroline Fixter and the staff at SHU Library and Sheffield Central Library for their endless research assistance. I must also thank Dr. Joachim Trinkwitz for maintaining an incredibly comprehensive comics research bibliography at the University of Bonn. And to Mikel Bermello Isusi and the staff at Ohio State University Library, who tracked down a cover image for me—big thanks!

Thank you to the many comics shops that have helped me to find material, especially Page 45 Nottingham, OK Comics Leeds, and Asylum Comics Aberdeen. I'm sure I'm getting a reputation for asking for weird stuff, but it's not a bad one to have. Support small comics shops!

I would like to thank my friends and colleagues for their assistance and encouragement: Dr. Jess Anderson, Ro Daniels,

Arabella Earle, Alex Fitch, Dr. Guy Lawley, Dr. Amy Matthewson, Dr. Christina Meyer, Dr. Mihaela Precup, Camilla Prince, Gabi Putnoki, Dr. Ana María Sánchez-Arce, Dr. Johannes Schmid, "The Scientits," Lucy Starbuck Braidley, Chris Sykes, Dr. Eszter Szép, and Dr. Laurike in 't Velt.

To Dr. Sasha Garwood Lloyd, who listened to me ramble on our wonderful walks along the Sheffield Canal and gave advice that was always kind, considered, and exactly what I needed.

To Steve and Anna. Steve, this is all your fault. This book wouldn't exist without you; I hope you approve! I look forward to celebrating it with you in person if the accident will . . . but perhaps not over a curry.

To Charmaine Townson, my sister from another mister. Charly, I love you, and you're the best friend I could have. Here's another for your collection.

And finally, as always, my never-ending thanks and love to Carsten and his indefatigable pompoms.

ABBREVIATIONS

ARVN   Army of the Republic of Vietnam—the official military force of South Vietnam

MAAG   Military Assistance Advisory Group—a group of U.S. military advisors sent to assist in the training of conventional armed forces and facilitate military aid

MACV   Military Assistance Command, Vietnam—joint-service command of the U.S. Department of Defense, composed of forces from the army, navy, and air force; created on February 8, 1962

MGR   mere gook rule—a racist "rule" that encouraged violence against any Vietnamese person, regardless of their political or military affiliation

MIA   missing in action

NLF   National Liberation Front—Vietnamese political organization aiming to overthrow the South Vietnamese government and reunify North and South Vietnam; formed on December 20, 1960

NVA   North Vietnamese Army—military force also known as the PAVN

PAVN   People's Army of Vietnam—national military force of the Socialist Republic of Vietnam and the armed wing of the ruling Communist Party of Vietnam (CPV)

PLAF   People's Liberation Armed Forces—also known as the Liberation Army of South Vietnam and the armed wing of the NLF

VC   Viet Cong—another name for the NLF but with a broader focus on South Vietnam, Laos, and Cambodia

VVAW   Vietnam Veterans against War—American antiwar organization founded in 1967

SILENCE IN THE QUAGMIRE

Introduction

The American War

> The picture of the world's greatest superpower killing or seriously injuring a thousand noncombatants a week, while trying to pound a tiny backward nation into submission on an issue whose merits are hotly disputed, is not a pretty one.
> —ROBERT MCNAMARA

The United States of America did not win the Vietnam War. On April 30, 1975, troops from the People's Army of Vietnam (PAVN) entered Saigon and captured key buildings. The flag of the National Liberation Front (NLF—alias Viet Cong / VC) was raised above the Independence Palace at 11:30 a.m. By 2:30 p.m. the South Vietnamese president, Dương Văn Minh, was announcing surrender on Radio Saigon. The takeover was swift and wholly expected by the United States; the evacuation of U.S. troops was already well underway. It was clear to all involved that the war had been won, and *not* by the world's strongest military; the United States had been forced to withdraw for good this time. But according to the statistics from the U.S. Department of Defense, the United States *was* winning. Secretary of Defense Robert McNamara was a notorious "number cruncher" who advocated for statistics and metrics to measure the success of the war. The primary data point was "kills" (i.e., dead enemies), but other metrics included tonnage of bombs dropped and square mileage of U.S.-controlled land. The general consensus was that using data to drive tactical decision-making removed the risks of bias, emotion, and personal conviction; it is worth mentioning here that McNamara was recruited to the Department of Defense after being president of the Ford Motor Company. But McNamara's scientific bean counting would only work if the raw data were accurate—which they were not. The defeat, therefore, was counter to what *should* have happened according to the data, and so while the United States looked good on paper, North Vietnam looked better on the ground. But is the winner of the war the one who controls the land or the one who controls the narrative? The United States may have lost the land, but their firm grip on the narrative of the conflict has only tightened in the five decades since the fall of Saigon.

By the nature of their form and publication contexts, comics have acted as a barometer of social and political opinion both during and since the war. This was not a new phenomenon during this conflict but has long been a lens through which we can view popular-culture artifacts. In 1937 V. F. Calverton wrote of culture as "history in evening dress, powdered, rouged, brow plucked, hair-coifed, diamond-ringed, ermine-sheathed, gliding on 'light fantastic toe,' eager to go places and do things."[1] For Calverton, culture exists in a "double capacity as a reflector and a barometer of history in process." Though he is speaking more generally of all levels of cultural output, his description of culture as something we may unkindly label as gaudy and transitory speaks directly to comics as a form. Writing of comics specifically, Martin Lund recognizes the barometric nature of the form in line with its publication contexts: "Mainstream comic books and, to a lesser extent, graphic novels, and other long-form comics, produced for a mass audience, often address current events and articulate what is perceived as the essence of the attitudes and sentiments of their time and place. By virtue of their being thus anchored in their immediate context and the immediacy with which they communicate, such comics can show us how their creators regarded the world in which they lived, how they maneuvered the identity-climate of their day, and how they conceived of their own place in the United States."[2] This immediacy of communication and context is seen in Vietnam War comics in the way that visual characterizations of Vietnamese characters change as the war itself developed; in the gap left by the erasure of women's labor; in the relegation of women and girls, when shown, to tightly defined and heavily stereotyped roles; and in the stereotyped portrayals of veterans.

This book is a study of the uses of silence in the construction of the Americentric narrative of the Vietnam War. This book is *not* a comprehensive study of all American comics of the war, and it does not pretend to be. That book would be far longer than this one, and it is a book that should be written. What this book aims to do, instead, is to focus on those voices that are excluded from the classic war narrative—which typically centers on white, working-class American servicemen and their experiences of combat. This book focuses on the less visible players: the Vietnamese on both sides of the conflict, women and girls, and returning veterans. I interrogate the ways in which this conflict is represented in American comic books, with special focus on these missing groups. I discuss how and, more importantly, why these groups are represented as they are, if at all, and the ways in which these representations have affected views of the war, both during and since. Using Foucault's understanding of silence as discourse, I consider the ways in which both silence and silencing are mobilized in the creation of the U.S.-centric war narrative.

It would be remiss of me to ignore the concept of soft power at this point. Though the concept itself is not new and such power has been levied by nations against nations for centuries, the term itself rose to popularity in the 1990s, after the publication of Joseph Nye's book *Bound to Lead: The Changing Nature of American Power*. Nye writes that "one country [getting] other countries to want what it wants might be called co-optive or soft power in contrast with the hard or command power of ordering others to do what it wants."[3] Soft power is not coercive; the currency is cultural output, foreign policy, and political change.[4] Indeed, the business-focused magazine *Monocle* publishes a "soft power survey" annually, including factors such as Olympic medals and the quality of a nation's architecture as indicators of soft power. During the Cold War, both the United States and the Soviet Union used markers of soft power to control their narratives and to persuade the world of the attractiveness of their own systems. Ultimately, the Soviets' closed system and lack of outward-facing popular culture impeded their ability to compete with the United States.[5] However, criticism of soft power has increased in international relations circles. Margaret Seymour suggests, "Soft power approaches are targeted toward human beings with all their individualistic complexity. . . . Preferences, beliefs, and societal norms are influenced by any number of factors, meaning the residents of a village outside of Nairobi are likely to react very differently to the same messaging as suburban dwellers outside of Chicago."[6] She cites the failure of the Shared Values Initiative (SVI), which was designed to strengthen pro-American feeling across the Muslim world in 2002. The initiative failed, in part, due to the lack of interagency coordination and openness to cross-disciplinary approaches.

Furthermore, soft power is very hard to quantify and therefore measure in terms of success. If a successful outcome is "changed attitudes," how does one effectively measure that?

Though the concept has been criticized, it remains a useful one for my purposes within this book. If the concept was, as Ilan Manor and Guy Golan suggest, a way that "America could make the world American without using weapons," then we can use it as a lens for viewing U.S. popular culture that actively engaged with a war that was, according to many, about stopping a communist takeover in Southeast Asia (and beyond).[7] These popular-culture artifacts can be seen as objects of soft power, not necessarily for consumption on an international level, but for strengthening the base of support on the home front

Linda Dittmar and Gene Michaud write that cinema gave the United States "the power to make images that place, distort, and destroy knowledge of the history in which those lives (and many others) participated."[8] Comics also held this power, with vast numbers of storylines disseminating views of the conflict that backed the government's position. The power of American publishing and cultural creation far outstripped anything that Vietnam was able to counter, both during the war and since, giving the United States a clear advantage to take control of the war's narrative.

The Vietnam War holds a difficult role in American memory and mythogenesis that has never been fully assimilated into the American national narrative. What comics about the war have striven to do is to reframe the war narrative in ways that make sense within the wider (American) national story: one of masculine heroism, military superiority, and a backstabbing U.S.-controlled government. In real terms, this becomes the silencing and exclusion of those who may complicate this narrative. The rest of this chapter gives a very brief history of comics of the war. I then discuss the concept and theory of silence.

How can comics be complicit in the pushing of exclusionary narratives of conflict that contribute to the marginalization of certain groups? How does the silence (or silencing) of these groups in the narrative affect the discourses of the war?

Drawing the War since 1950

The war in Vietnam that eventually became known as the Vietnam War had started many years before the United States arrived in the country. Indeed, the official start date remains a matter of debate. It was only in 1998 that the U.S. Department of Defense (DoD) designated it as November 1, 1955. On this date, the U.S. Military Assistance Advisory Group (MAAG), which had been deployed under President Truman in 1950, was reorganized and MAAG Vietnam was established.[9] While it is not my goal in this book to explain the entire timeline of the war, I mention this here to highlight two things: first, that five decades after its end, this conflict is still the topic of debate on some of its most fundamental facts and, second, to explain my starting point when considering comics of the war.

In the early 1950s, the United States was embroiled in war in Korea. As Leonard Rifas notes in his expansive study, not only did war comics present an often-nuanced version of the Korean War, but also the Korean War proved to be a turning point in terms of how war stories, in general, were told in comics.[10] Rifas emphasizes that "because American soldiers have not fought on American soil in living memory, people in the U.S. depend to an unusually large degree on media images to understand the realities of war," something that would be amplified in Vietnam by the almost constant televisual and photographic news coverage.[11] Beyond that, the future of the comics industry itself was not stable. The 1950s comics industry was embroiled in a heated fight against censorship, which most famously led to the Comics Code Authority and the death of several genres, regardless of their high levels of readership and intense popularity.[12] David Huxley reminds us that the "attack on comics by various critics which subsequently led to censorship did not concentrate in the main on war comics" but that they were not immune to criticism.[13] In 1954 Geoffrey Wagner wrote, "Battle dotes on action.... Hooray for the Brooklyn Dodgers! he yells as he plunges his bayonet hilt-deep in yet another red.... It is all gorgeous carnage, topped off with a joke or two in dreadful taste."[14] The "gorgeous carnage" ended with the implementation of the CCA; instead, gore was replaced by bullets and gunfire that killed without blood. Of this same period of comics, Rifas writes, "War comics struggled on, but on a smaller scale. As the bitterness of the Korean War faded from memory, most comic book stories set against that background celebrated military heroism and minimized the horrors even further. The remaining U.S. war comics focused their attention mainly on World War II in Western Europe, and the most commercially successful war comics of the 1960s featured characters whose names in the title assured their survival from one issue to the next: Sgt. Rock and Sgt. Fury."[15]

It was into this unstable and struggling industry that the first comic to feature conflict in Vietnam—still called Indochina at this point—was printed in *Wings Comics* 120 in the summer of 1953.[16] "The Raiders' Roost" follows two U.S. Air Force (USAF) pilots, Chuck Warren and John Stevens, as they search for "murder-MIGs." The two Americans witness Việt Minh soldiers desecrating a shrine. While attempting to stop the Việt Minh soldiers, the U.S. pilots are ambushed, and Stevens is shot down. A group of escaped French POWs arrive to save Stevens, and the day is saved with a little extra help by some USAF jets. "The Raiders' Roost" is in many ways a typical war story of the early 1950s. Both pilots were Korean War vets, and the conflict in Indochina was viewed as an extension of Korea, against the communist menace. The Red menace is emphasized through the terms "[Việt Minh] rebels" and "Red robots."[17] This is—to the best of my knowledge—the first comic of the war, and it put in place many of the conventions that have proved difficult to shake off. Furthermore, it was published before the majority of Americans would have had much, if any, knowledge of the existence of the conflict itself.

On July 21, 1954, the International Geneva Conference granted independence to Vietnam, Laos, and Cambodia, while also dividing Vietnam along the seventeenth parallel. The French colonial presence left the country, having been recently defeated by the Việt Minh at Điện Biên Phủ, and the regime in South Vietnam was supported by the U.S. military. Stories about the ground war in Vietnam had already been published—in early 1954, *before* the Geneva Conference. As with "The Raiders' Roost" the year prior, "Indo-China Raid" showed shadowy "Asian" fighters facing plucky and skilled Americans.[18] Early Vietnam stories followed well-worn paths of war as shown in conventional battle spaces; this was set to change quickly as the war became a "war without fronts." Yet these stories were in no way accurate, as shown by the depiction of Việt Minh aircraft (which did not exist at this time—North Vietnam did not have aircraft until 1964) and the U.S. soldiers' arrival by tank (which would have been impossible at the time).

In general, reading war comics requires us to suspend disbelief. Though their renderings of military hardware were often highly detailed, these comics are guided by the supra-ideology of entertainment, though they were extremely useful as propaganda, too. Prior to 1968, when the war would take a decisive (and, for the United States and South Vietnam, catastrophic) shift, comics were fanciful and often ridiculous. They favored the U.S. support of South Vietnam and, for the most part, suggested that the United States was doing a very good job.

To most readers, Vietnam remained an abstract place that could be shown visually as any place in Southeast Asia. They believed that the United States was holding the country together, supporting an army who were unable to work effectively on their own, with U.S. assistance offering the means if not the motive for the South Vietnamese to "grow up." By far, the most popular and prolific publishers of this period were Dell and Charlton, who published *Fightin' Army* (1956–84), *Fightin' Air Force* (1956–66), *Fightin' Marines* (1955–84), *Fightin' Navy* (1956–84), and *Jungle War Stories* (1962–65), along with other more imaginatively titled war books.

Despite their prolific output, Charlton was "a comparatively minor company . . . a kind of bargain basement company who paid low rates to contributors and were particularly badly printed in a field not noted for its excellence of production."[19] Quality of the publications did not matter to the large number of eager readers; according to Bradford Wright, these two publishers "expounded an unqualified endorsement of U.S. intervention."[20]

Despite their many titles, Charlton did not publish a sustained run of Vietnam stories, instead choosing to mix stories about several conflicts in each issue. However, Dell did opt for a sustained title—in *Jungle War Stories*. Starting in the spring of 1962, the first issue was a broad war comic, which then settled into a series of eleven issues that focused on Vietnam. One issue opened with a bold statement to the reader: "While the territory currently considered in the possession of South Vietnam is placed at more than one-half Vietnam's total area of 125,000 square miles . . . this figure is true only for the daylight hours. At night—when its guerrillas roam the land at will—it is estimated that North Vietnam actually controls more than 70 per cent of the Nation!"[21] South Vietnam was pictured as a corrupt, collapsing country, run by men plagued by the traditional, racist trope of Asiatic hubris and cowardice. Three grizzled Korean War veterans—Captain Duke Larsen, Sergeant "Cactus" Kane, and "G.I." Mike Williams—are charged with training members of the ARVN but always end up engaged in combat, involving increasingly bizarre stories—one involved fighting off the NLF with an ice machine and ended, in typical fashion, with Duke Larsen quipping, "See those monkeys scramble! They look as if they are going to retreat all the way back to Hanoi."[22]

In pre-1965 comics, the war was largely interpreted as an insurgency using guerrilla tactics; while this may have been partly correct, it reflected a much broader misunderstanding of the conflict. The war was not one of Communism *versus* democracy but a far more nuanced, multigenerational conflict that placed the desire for a unified Vietnam after many years of colonial presence in dialogue with resistance to the repressive Diệm regime. Labeling the NLF as "thugs" erased the complex political roots and linked cleanly with the perception of Communism as an ideology of violence and injustice. By 1965 the NLF could boast that they controlled roughly 60 percent of South Vietnam, which is only slightly less than the number given in *Jungle War Stories* 7 the previous year.

In November 1963 ARVN generals deposed and assassinated President Ngô Đình Diệm in a coup supported by the United States. A few weeks later, John F. Kennedy was also assassinated, elevating Lyndon B. Johnson to president. The United States was sinking deeper into the "quagmire" of the war. More and more personnel were entering Vietnam, and the role of the United States was no longer advisory. War comics could not maintain their whimsical jungle stories. The enemy had become a real and immediate threat to American servicemen, and the war could no longer be presented as uncontroversial.

The antiwar protests had begun; the first draft-card burning happened on May 12, 1964.

Charlton presented themselves as the publisher who not only would give informed, accurate information about the war but would also publish comics in "real time" as the war progressed. "A New Kind of War" presented a brief history of the American soldier in the twentieth century. It is a curious text that erases any of the violent past of the United States—indeed, any combat before 1914 is seemingly missing. The "doughboys in France had to learn ... and the experts in Germany, France, and England smiled at [their] first efforts."[23] Ignoring the blatant errors in this depiction of the United States as a naive yet remarkably war-capable juvenile nation, the comic continues in a similar vein to suggest that "the doughboys learned" and that "in the end they were as good or better at this grisly skill as any nationality!" The comic concludes that, ultimately, Vietnam is a "strange land" that requires a "new kind of war" that the United States will learn and that even though "[they]'ve lost some men and [they]'ll lose some more," the United States will kill large numbers of Vietnamese. This show of patriotism does not necessarily end on a positive note but is at least successful in showing that Vietnam was not the sort of war that the United States had fought previously.

Comics could not ignore the growing "Americanization" of the war, nor the shift from advisory presence to direct combatants. The focus shifted from elite forces sent to train the ARVN and instead focused on regular soldiers and marines. The comics coverage mimicked to a large extent the war that was being broadcast into the homes of American television viewers each evening on news programs; Michael Mandelbaum emphasizes that Vietnam was the first "televised" war.[24] Like television viewers, comics readers wanted to follow "regular soldiers." The enemy remained elusive, a devious and deadly foe who hid in jungles and tunnels, fighting by sneak attack. Story arcs such as "Ghost Battalion" in *Army War Heroes* 14 (1966) and "The New Breed" in *War Heroes* 23 (1967) featured a hidden, wily enemy that was as dangerous as he was elusive. The "new kind of war" was here.

Most comics in the early to mid-1960s continued in this vein; a notable exception, "Landscape," appeared in the antiwar comic *Blazing Combat* in 1966. The story centers on a Vietnamese village attacked by U.S. forces. An aging rice farmer reflects on the military presence and is eventually killed, despite playing no role in the conflict. The series publisher, James Warren, was aware that the comic might not be as popular as other war titles, due to its firm antiwar stance. Warren stated in an interview, "Here is my distributor, saying, 'Uh oh! Wait until our wholesalers—many of them belonging to the American Legion—see this!' They found out very fast that it was anti-war."[25] "Landscape" ran in the second issue; because of it, "American PX shops (shops set up on American military bases internationally) refused to stock it."[26] Though this was not the final death knell of the comic series, it did mark its decline. Warren states, "And the story that I got back was that the American Legion, which was very much gung-ho for Vietnam or any conflict involving American boys at that time, looked on us and saw us as traitors to our own country. And I think that happened with the second issue. The sales were terrible. They were terrible with the third and, of course, they were terrible with the fourth."[27] Though the storyline of "Landscape" is distinctly different from other war comics of the same era, the antiwar sentiment comes through, not so much via explicit statements against war, but in the raw honesty of the narrative—the presentation of an innocent protagonist caught up in the conflict and the depiction of American action that was not necessarily by the book. By contemporary standards, "Landscape" is not bold; by 1960s standards, especially given that comics publication was governed by the CCA's strict guidelines, as mentioned earlier, and that one of the main markets was the military, it was shocking. Similar antiwar works were not seen on the newsstands during the war; they appeared much later. Even then, the focus was not placed squarely on the Vietnamese experience.

In one of the most misguided statements of the entire war, General Westmoreland declared, "I am absolutely certain that whereas in 1965 the enemy was winning, today he is certainly losing."[28] He made this statement in November 1967; in January 1968 the NLF launched the Tet Offensive. Though the withdrawal of troops was still several years away, the war was entering a long and drawn-out endgame. During this time, a shift in focus happened across the board. Even Charlton, who had previously touted themselves as representing the actual war, shifted. By the late 1960s, the action hero had replaced the soldier. Charlton did still offer some small contribution to debates surrounding the war, especially the "hawk-and-dove" conversations;[29] their offering was a chicken—Private "Chicken" Smith to be exact.

During the post-Tet period, it was Charlton's *Fightin' Marines* that produced the largest number of Vietnam stories in American war comics. These were still not a single, cohesive series that focused on the war itself, but several story arcs over the course of the series. Several of these arcs featured Sergeant "Shotgun" Harker and his nervous, effeminate sidekick, Private "Chicken" Smith, who was depicted with flowers in his helmet. They were often found wandering in the jungle at the beginning of a story and habitually became separated from their company. Despite the odd-couple pairing, many of the story arcs were remarkably sensitive to contemporaneous attitudes toward the war. One such arc showed a corporal in extreme psychological distress. Harker states, "One of the worst ways a Marine can get hurt is inside his head ... they can't bandage it or put on a splint, but the wounds are just as serious. Yah get nicked in the finger or an ear, they give ya a Purple Heart ... but if you blow your mind, ya get nothin'!"[30] Such comments clearly echoed the views expressed by many thousands of returned veterans and a huge swath of the American public. On one level, the series conformed to the wider trends in Vietnam War comics. First, while the pair of marines often found themselves fighting the enemy as part of a larger formation, they often became separated or simply began the story wandering through the Vietnamese hinterland on their own. While oddly matched and certainly not Special Forces, the duo represented a variation of the one-man-army trope. However, by this point the war was lost. In 1969 the United States started to withdraw ground support; in January 1973 both North and South Vietnam, along with the United States, signed the Paris Peace Accords. The war was finally over on April 30, 1975, when Saigon fell.

As the war was playing out nightly on television news, there was little appetite for film or sustained comics narratives; only one film was released during the war—*The Green Berets*, starring John Wayne and released in 1968. As I have shown, comics *did* engage with the conflict, but there was no single comics series released during this time. It was only after the war that longer Vietnam narratives in their own dedicated series began to appear. Huxley suggests that the lack of Vietnam stories is purely economic—they did not sell well. Reitberger and Fuchs write that "the Vietnam War is much too controversial for an all-out engagement," and this does appear to be a significant factor in the death of Vietnam stories during this time.[31]

According to Viet Thanh Nguyen, all wars are "fought twice, first on the battlefield, then in memories." He writes that this is true of the Vietnam War and describes "the industry of memory" as "[incorporating] the processes of individual memory, the collective nature of its making, and the social contexts of its meanings."[32] For Nguyen, Hollywood as an industry has the power to control the war narrative through its films, which is no less true of comics. The meaning and sense making that began in Hollywood in the late 1970s can be seen in the range of comics published since 1975, which, like their televisual cousins, "strive to find something redeeming to say about this war even as they echo the public's myriad and often contradictory misgivings about it."[33]

There are only two substantial comics series set entirely during the war: *The 'Nam* and *Vietnam Journal*.[34] Both series have a stable cast of characters, allowing them to develop character arcs and establish relationships between characters, as well as between character and place. *Vietnam Journal*, written by Don Lomax and published between 1987 and 1991, follows Scott "Journal" Neithammer, a war correspondent embedded with several platoons. Journal is dedicated to showing the war as it really is; he often places himself in dangerous situations, narrowly escaping serious injury or death on several occasions. He distinguishes himself from other journalists by his openness to the realities of the war, including helping a woman to deliver a baby at one point. Lomax was drafted in 1965 and served with the Ninety-Eighth Light Equipment Company. Many of the sketches and notes he made during his tour were incorporated into the series. According to Lomax, the war "opened my eyes. Before I went into the war, I trusted everybody, and when I came out, I trusted nobody or the government."[35] This antipathy to war is clear in the series.

In contrast to the grit of *Vietnam Journal*, the creators of *The 'Nam* emphasized the series' ethos, which saw it as being a comic written within the guidelines of the CCA and focused on average soldiers. Elsewhere, I have written of *The 'Nam*,

INTRODUCTION 15

"The constraints of both CCA and Marvel's 'house style' combined create a text that ignores many aspects of the soldiers' experience of Vietnam (notably swearing and drug usage) but does not stifle representations of the intense trauma that many endured."[36] Series creator Doug Murray said in an interview that he "wanted a way to at least tell a part of the story to the kids and maybe get other people to talk about it as well."[37] Despite aspects of the conflict that are absent due to censorship, "*The 'Nam* helped reinvigorate the war comic genre."[38]

In the first issue of *The 'Nam*, Murray claims that he wrote the series with the aim "to give a realistic portrayal of the war."[39] The series ran for eight years, from 1986 to 1993, and follows a rigid structure that mimics the standard U.S. Army tour of duty of 366 days in theater. Throughout the run, the writers place characters into actual historical events without causing disruption to the comic's timescale. This has the effect of grounding the story arcs in historical landmarks familiar to the reader, creating narrative touchstones that also give credence to Murray's attempts at realism. The mimicking of the 366-day tour lets the reader develop a relationship with the characters in a similar way to their fellow soldiers, which would be lost if characters cycled in and out of the series more rapidly. Robert Kodosky notes that "Vietnam War comics consistently depict small cohesive platoons threatened by outside forces."[40] This is the model followed by *The 'Nam*. Though the primary focus of the first thirteen issues is Private Ed Marks, he exists within the platoon as an equal participant in all events. The positioning of Marks provides a "handle" for the reader—a character onto whom we can latch to move through the narrative and place ourselves within the platoon's internal relationships.

Halfway through its eighty-four-issue run, *The 'Nam* ran a single issue that "guest starred" Iron Man, Captain America, and Thor. *The 'Nam* 41 ("Back in the Real World") is a fanciful and almost naive answer to the question: What if superheroes were in Vietnam? In an earlier issue, Private Aeder is killed, leaving behind a stack of comics. Another soldier, nicknamed Iceman, finds them and begins to read them nostalgically. He imagines Thor, Captain America, and Iron Man working together to capture Ho Chi Minh and fly him to Paris to negotiate a settlement. Iceman and Martini laugh over these comics, making it clear they know that such scenarios are pure fiction. The ending of the comic undercuts this mood of realism by returning to the glorious heroism that characterizes the vast majority of superhero narratives. As two soldiers watch Iceman's helicopter leave, the faces of Iron Man, Cap, and Thor appear in the clouds. One soldier comments, "Iceman doesn't think there are heroes anymore!" and receives the reply, "Real heroes rarely think of themselves as anything special."[41] In positioning Iceman in the same visual area as the superheroes he is afforded a distinctly American (and distinctly comics) heroism that undercuts any attempt at realistic presentation and replaces it with saccharine Manicheanism. *The 'Nam*'s creators are playing on a generalized, nostalgic version of superheroes as undoubtedly good, and this framing is used to impute an indisputable goodness and rightness to Iceman and his brothers-in-arms.

Other preexisting series began to retcon their characters into Vietnam. Some were set in theater, while others tackled the characters' postwar experiences. In many cases, this made sense, given the characters' backstories. In the early 1990s, *The 'Nam* ran two mini arcs in which Frank Castle (aka the Punisher) was deployed in Vietnam.[42] Both arcs position Castle as an elite soldier who must single-handedly fight an elite Vietnamese soldier and a drug dealer to restore the power of the U.S. military. Castle's guest appearance is part of an attempt to reinvigorate the series and to draw in new readers. While there may have been a crossover in the readership of *The 'Nam* and *The Punisher*, here it became explicit. Castle exists within the narrative and character relationships already existing in *The 'Nam*. In later comics, especially *The Punisher: Born* (2011) and *Punisher: The Platoon* (2017), he reenters Vietnam, and the reader learns that the character "was in fact born on a battlefield overseas and not thanks to a domestic tragedy that occurred stateside after his military service ended."[43]

Frank Castle is not the only character to be retconned into a Vietnam veteran. Nick Fury is given similar treatment in *Fury: My War Gone By* (2013) and *Get Fury* (2024). Across thirteen issues, the comic follows Fury's time in the military, beginning in the 1950s in Indochina, working with the CIA, and then to Cuba in 1961, before returning to Vietnam in 1970, at the height of American intervention.[44] The narrative divorces Fury from his typical role within Marvel's superhero-filled universe and S.H.I.E.L.D., instead being set in "real-world" scenarios. In a sense, the character returns to his roots, as Fury debuted in *Sgt. Fury and His Howling Commandos* (which ran from 1963 to 1981) while also appearing in *Strange Tales* as a CIA superspy (from 1965 onward).

Comics like *Fury: My War Gone By* are entirely fictional, despite their setting in recognizable locations and using historical events as touchstones. In the twenty-first century, the rise in popularity of autographics—life writing in comics form—has created space for true stories about Vietnam to be written by those who experienced them or, more commonly, those whose families experienced them. Two of these life narratives are written by names more commonly associated with other types of comics: *Last Day in Vietnam: A Memory* (2000) by Will Eisner and *Dong Xoai, Vietnam 1965* (2011) by Joe Kubert. Both men were above the age of the draft by the time the war began, so they were not involved in combat. Eisner made several trips to Southeast Asia for *PS: The Preventive Maintenance Monthly*, for which he was artistic director between 1951 and 1971. In 2000 he published a collection of the short stories he had drawn during these trips, all of which show "soldiers who are engaged not only in the daily hostilities of war but also in larger, more personal combat."[45]

While Kubert and Eisner were too old to fight in Vietnam, Derf Backderf was too young. Despite him not taking part in the war beyond viewing it on television, Backderf's 2020 comic *Kent State: Four Dead in Ohio* presents a clear and necessary version of the first few days of May 1970 (Friday, May 1, to Monday, May 4) and the events surrounding the Kent State massacre.[46] For Backderf, "the massacre is far more than the events of the 4th in isolation, but the inevitable culmination of a long weekend of protests and riots, in an era already marred by socio-political instability."[47] The comic places the iconic death of Jeffrey Miller within the wider—and extremely complex—context of the national protest events, the national student strike of May 1, and the atmosphere of unrest and surveillance that pervades this period. In an interview with the *Journal of Graphic Novels and Comics*, Backderf states, "I made it about the four kids. When they are cut down, and I show exactly how they were cut down, it really is a gut punch for the reader. There was no reason for it to happen. It was completely inexplicable. All of these great political forces of the era came crashing together in that one place."[48] Backderf's comic fills out the narrative of a massacre that many only know as a single, horrible photograph: the image of a dead Jeffrey Miller and a screaming Mary Ann Vecchio. His comic creates space to tell the full story of that day. It is a corrective intervention into the accepted narrative, though one that is still dependent on a U.S. point of view.

As I discuss in the conclusion of this book, these interventions are becoming more common as family narratives that give a multifaceted, nuanced view of the war are being created and published. Viet Thanh Nguyen calls the war "more than just an object in the rearview mirror" of American cultural memory, adding that "[it is] over, but its visual images live on."[49] This is seen most clearly in *Vietnamerica: A Family's Journey* (2010) by GB Tran and *The Best We Could Do* (2017) by Thi Bui, both of whom contrast versions of the classic U.S.-centric military narrative of Vietnam, using their own family histories to reposition the Vietnamese as central players in the conflict and create a narrative that demonstrates the costs of the war on the ordinary citizens of Vietnam. In resituating the conflict in the villages and daily lives of the Vietnamese, giving agency to Vietnamese characters, and representing this mostly unspoken side of the conflict, Tran and Bui are able to crack open the shell protecting the U.S.-centric representation of Vietnam. For them, the Vietnam War is not just a military interaction between national players that occurred between 1955 and 1975. It is part of the enduring history of their families' homes and their own personal identity constructions. I return to these two comics in the conclusion.

Silence and the War

In this text, I focus on voices that are largely missing from the war narrative, demonstrating how comics can be complicit in the pushing of exclusionary narratives that contribute to the marginalization of certain groups. Marginalization and exclusion are rendered as silence within the comic: characters that do not speak and are not visually present and topics that are not addressed. Silence itself becomes a key framework for reading and interpreting these comics texts. For Michel Foucault, silence is "less the absolute limit of discourse ... than an element that functions alongside the things said, with them and in relation to them within overall strategies."[50] The silences that these comics contain are therefore a part of the text. This lens allows me to consider the silence of—and about—these groups as a part of the discourse of the war and to ask how this lens affects the U.S.-centric war narrative. How does the silence (or silencing) of these groups in the narrative affect the discourses of the war?

As Foucault writes, "There is not one but many silences, and they are an integral part of the strategies that underlie and permeate discourses."[51] There are distinct differences among these many silences, in their expression, effect, and power. Charles de Gaulle famously stated that "silence is the ultimate weapon of power"—while this may bring to mind a figure of quiet strength, where the frantic need to speak is replaced with confidence and conviction, "one could also read that to mean that the silence of the ruled strengthens the ruler."[52] Here, silence becomes a privilege of the powerful.

Silence can be a weapon against oppression, a tool for the oppressed to fight without words, their presence itself a protest. In Herman Melville's 1853 short story "Bartleby, the Scrivener," the titular character slowly descends into near silence and inaction within his employer's offices, eventually becoming mute and starving to death in a New York prison.[53] As an employee trapped within the capitalist system, Bartleby's body and voice are his only properties and tools that only he can control. In denying access to these tools, he is making a statement of protest and removing himself from the capitalist system while remaining physically within it, a decision that perplexes both his employer and colleagues. Bartleby's silence is by active choice. However, within the corpus I tackle in this book, we do not see this self-silencing. Though there are many examples of self-silencing within conflict situations—such as refusing to speak after capture, to avoid giving information to the enemy or to protect one's comrades—there are no examples of this in my corpus. This type of silence requires (and demands) agency; the characters in my corpus have none.

While choosing not to speak can be an act of strength and defiance, being silenced strips the individual or group of their agency and power. We may see it as an act of violence against a marginalized group, governed and controlled by a comparatively small group of speakers. This violent silencing is not solely the responsibility of the military; the media is equally complicit. In Vietnam these speakers were overwhelmingly American. Norman Solomon writes, "[The United States] has grown acclimated to the implicit assumptions wrapped in daily news, punditry, and pronouncements from government officials. What happens at the other end of American weaponry has remained almost entirely a mystery, with only occasional brief glimpses before the curtain falls back into its usual place."[54] The silencing of victims in Vietnam began quickly, as "very little footage of the suffering and death got on the air."[55] Even as it was playing out in-country, the military and media began the process of silencing victim voices—both Vietnamese and American—and controlling the narrative to build the televised view that eventually became the mononarrative as understood by millions of Americans. According to Edward Jay Epstein's analysis of news coverage, "producers of the NBC and ABC Evening News programs said that they ordered editors to delete excessively grisly or detailed shots because they were not appropriate for a news program shown at dinnertime."[56] The president of CBS claimed that the networks aimed to "shield the audience from the true horror of the war."[57] Even the definition of war itself was created in such a way that a huge swath of the experience of conflict was rendered invisible: "For the American [media] networks, 'war' means troops on the ground in harm's way."[58]

If invisibility is the visual cognate of silence, then the removal of characters from image narratives of the war is their silence.

Of course, the two must be closely related, because a character who is not physically there cannot speak. On the comics page, the two go hand in hand, as voice and image combine to present the U.S. military in terms that fit with both the official military and overarching media narratives. The groups I discuss in this book have long been divested of their power—by the colonial presence that took hold of governance in-country for many years; by patriarchy due to their gender; and by significant injury to both body and mind brought on by their time in combat, all of which have led to their silencing and invisibility. Speaking in terms of the prevailing narrative of the war as constructed in American popular culture, Keith Beattie considers not only the nonpresence of these groups but furthermore the silencing of any voice that does not offer "authentic experience": "Only those 'who were there' (that is, who took part in the war) are legitimated to speak of the experience. As commonly represented, only men existed in Vietnam. Women, therefore, were not allowed to speak since, according to the logic of popular definitions, they were not there."[59] Even though these groups *were* there—and in the case of Vietnamese characters, had been there for centuries—their difference from the default figure of "white inarticulate men" erases them and reduces their very real actions within the war to invisibility.[60] This book views these different silent groups together under the auspices of the preeminent narrative of the Vietnam War, which creates silence as a site of power, oppression, and dominance. The lens of silencing has many applications within comics studies. For comics of war and conflict, as more storylines are created that focus on more recent conflicts, such as the Gulf Wars and the War on Terror, an awareness of the visual erasure and silencing that is at play can be used to highlight how U.S.-centric comics narratives are enacting narrative damage by ignoring a large swath of the voices of the conflict. In these conflicts especially, the focus so far has been on American servicemen in the theater, without any characters of the home nations, similar to the material produced about Vietnam. Even in conflicts with huge numbers of different comics and an equally large output of scholarship, the existence of a dominant focus necessarily silences certain voices. We see this, for example, in Second World War comics, where the voices of civilians are lost in the noise of soldiers. It occurs in comics of the Holocaust, where only now the voices of Roma and Sinti people are being captured in comics form and scholarship. In reclaiming their stories, these victims and survivors of conflict violence are able to reclaim the power that is inherent in storytelling and identity creation through narrative.

Outside of war and conflict comics, comics scholarship has focused heavily on narratives of migration, movement of peoples, and diaspora. Gayatri Spivak asks, "Can the subaltern speak?"[61] Yes, they can, and in recognizing both the value of their words on the basic level of humans telling their own story and their importance to the overall narrative, comics scholarship will be well placed to make necessary interventions into storytelling and mythmaking as created, used, and mobilized by disparate groups of people as they move internationally and for myriad reasons. In laying out a framework that focuses on how these voices are erased—and shows what exists of them in place of accurate, nuanced representation—this book demonstrates not only that narratives of conflict and of people are poorer for having such gaps but also that there are ways to bring these missing voices to the fore.

Before moving on to the concluding part of this introduction, there is one final aspect of silencing to consider: the naming of the conflict. The name that we choose to know the conflict by is directly related, not only to the narrative that is put forward but to whom that narrative focuses on and who is ignored by it. As David Anderson explains, "The name 'Vietnam War' is the term most Americans use to denote the conflict that involved the United States in Indochina from about 1950 to 1975. Like the name, the dates are approximate."[62] However, this term narrows the space of the war to one country; when, in fact, the fighting and logistics of the war spread over at least three: Vietnam, Cambodia, and Laos. More accurate in terms of both dates and geographic scope would be the First and Second Indochina Wars, the first spanning from 1945 to 1954 and the second from 1960 to 1975. But none of these terms are those used by the Vietnamese themselves for their own conflict. Both the Vietnam War and the First and Second Indochina Wars are terms that are used primarily by the West (especially the United States and France) to describe conflicts that they participated in. Within Vietnam, the conflict has several names, most commonly *Kháng chiến chống Mỹ* (which translates to "Resistance War against America"). In conversations about the conflict, I have also heard terms including "the American War" and "Our War."[63] While this book does not perform a close analysis of the names used for the conflict, instead using the U.S. standard term "the Vietnam War," I note this here to highlight how the erasing of certain voices and perspectives is central to any discussion of the conflict. The choice of name immediately begins to lay the groundwork for the narrative that will be told. In the comics I discuss here, the erasure of multifaceted narratives in favor of a U.S.-centric one is made clear by their ignorance of any other name.

Chapter Breakdown

This book is divided into three chapters, each of which focuses on a different group that is either silent or silenced within the wider narrative of the war. Chapter 1 places the focus on the Vietnamese and their characterization as "the enemy." In a conflict that is, at its root, a civil war, the lines between enemy and ally are blurred. The silencing of Vietnamese voices contributes to this blurring by denying them any chance to speak for themselves. By giving no space to Vietnamese voices, the United States controls the whole narrative of the war, despite it being a civil war and one that the United States entered initially only as advisors. I consider the development of visual stereotypes of Southeast Asian people in the Western (especially American) press and how these impacted comics representations of the Vietnam War. As this book demonstrates, the volume of comics that include some depiction of the war is vast and the ways in which Vietnamese characters are portrayed ranges from an invisible force marked only by gunfire from the jungle to main characters given clear and nuanced character arcs. Tracing the spectrum of representation of the Vietnamese from awkward racist caricatures to more rounded characters is not a chronological endeavor. Though it is possible to suggest that earlier comics were more given to stereotyping, this is not strictly true, and there are many more recent publications that fall back on these visual tropes.

Chapter 2 shifts focus to women and girls. Where do they feature within these comics and in what roles? I view female characters through three distinct lenses: the caregiver, the combatant, and the commodity. To what extent do female characters fill these three roles? And what does this mean for representations of both femininity and masculinity in these comics? As women's roles in the U.S. military have changed and developed, so too has their position within popular-culture representations. I interrogate the extent to which this comes through in comics and, furthermore, how this can be measured alongside other cultural and sociopolitical changes relating to gender positionality in the wider world.

The final chapter moves away from figures in direct combat and instead centers on those who made it home. The returning soldier—the veteran—is not a common character type but is a familiar one across American popular-culture forms, especially film and television. Where they are shown, it is most commonly as drug-addled and violent "crazy vets." The figure of the soldier in theater is a key figure in popular culture, but the returned veteran is mostly ignored. And when the depictions are present, they follow a narrow model that is both instantly recognizable and mostly inaccurate. This chapter addresses the direct representation and erasure of traumatized veterans, while also considering the wider representation of trauma at play in comics about Vietnam. One aspect of trauma theory that is central to this chapter is the Freudian and post-Freudian idea that trauma is "unspeakable" and that traumatized soldiers are rendered silent by the psychological mechanisms of trauma. This idea therefore sits at the center of the veterans' silence: it is not that they are being silenced by external forces but rather by the trauma within.

1

Visualizing the Vietnamese

Monkeys, Monsters, and the Missing

We have met the enemy and he is us.

—WALT KELLY (1970)

In 1970 the syndicated comic character Pogo the Possum offered a grim indictment of the state of the world as part of an Earth Day strip. As the possum looks in horror at the trash in the Okefenokee Swamp, he turns to Porky Pine and speaks the words, "We have met the enemy and he is us."[1] His words spoof those of American naval officer Oliver Hazard Perry, who, after capturing Royal Navy ships in the 1813 Battle of Lake Erie, wrote the message, "We have met the enemy and they are ours."[2] Though Walt Kelly's immediate comment relates to environmentalism and the destruction of the planet by deliberate low-level action, such as littering and illegal dumping, it is hard not to see the parallels to Vietnam. By the time this strip was printed in 1970, nearly twenty million gallons of defoliants (including the highly carcinogenic herbicide Agent Orange) had been sprayed across the previously lush jungle landscape; at that point, the human cost of chemical warfare was not known. It has subsequently been linked to many congenital medical conditions, as well as cancer; Agent Orange has become one of the defining weapons of the war.[3]

But to read the comic without the environmental message brings to the fore two aspects of the conflict. First, the negative actions of the U.S. military led to their subsequent disavowal by the American public, a process that was well underway by 1970. Second, and far more difficult to pin down, the enemy was *not* a known quantity in Vietnam. The battle lines are steeped in decades of local and family histories, as well as several centuries of colonial occupation and geopolitical movement. The likelihood that the leaders of any foreign nation, let alone one with such drastically different social and cultural mores, would be able to grasp these contexts within a few short years of warfare is low. It is even less likely that the nuances of appearance and language would be comprehensible to an incoming foreign military. And it is in this environment that we find fertile ground for the planting of long-held racial and ethnic stereotypes, as well as the growth of new ones.

This chapter considers the visual and thematic representational strategies at play when presenting "the enemy." I interrogate the extent to which the Vietnamese are constructed as enemy in line with negative characteristics—an "enemy image," to use a phrase popularized by scholars including Jerome Frank and Andrei Melville as well as Janet Gross Stein. There is a distinct difference between the existence of an enemy and the "enemy image." According to Frank and Melville, *exclusively* negative moral characteristics will be used for depictions of the enemy in media coverage of conflicts. The image that is given to the media, therefore, lacks nuance and the characteristics of humanness that we all bear. Any sense of the histories and personal contexts of the enemy are lost, and what remains is an amorphous blob of evil dressed up in a shell constructed from visual stereotypes. Much of the rationale for the enemy image can be discussed in relation to cultural, racial, or nationalist "othering," as well as justification for military secrecy, covert action, or witch hunts.[4] But more than that, it is a highly effective method of silencing. By controlling perceptions of groups deemed the "enemy" in military discussions and wider public opinions via the media, these groups are silenced. Though this phenomenon is not unique to the war in Vietnam, there is an additional factor at play: the silencing through stereotype and enemy image was applied to *all* Vietnamese, including the U.S. allies in the South Vietnamese government and the ARVN. As I show later in this chapter, the perception of *all* Vietnamese as "gook" and therefore "enemy" was deeply ingrained.

The first part of this chapter considers the development of visual stereotypes of Southeast Asian people in the Western (especially American) press and how these impacted comics representations of the Vietnam War. In the second part, I move to specific examples of the different modes and tropes of representation used within these comics. I suggest that there are two broad categories into which the vast majority of depictions fit: simian creatures that are characterized by animalistic appearance and behaviors or missing, conspicuous by their absence and, if seen at all, reduced to a shadow or a burst of gunfire. Why are these characters reduced to beasts, if they exist at all; or if they aren't depicted, where are they? My corpus is divided into three distinct sections by chronology. I begin with comics that were published during the war (from 1955 to 1975). How was the enemy portrayed while the war was ongoing—would a single stereotyped portrayal suffice or were the depictions more nuanced? Then I look at comics of the postwar period, from 1975 to 2000; this was an era in which the U.S. military was not at war and there was focus on healing and trauma. How did this affect comics and the enemy? I close with post-2001 comics. This is the first period of the United States being at war since Vietnam, but the face of "the enemy" is distinctly different, as the enemy is portrayed in, comparatively, more nuanced and human ways.

Making the "Other" Visible

It is important to note at this juncture that the racial and racist dimensions of the Vietnam War did not begin with this conflict but were a part of the much wider discussion of race in Asian-American relations. Edward Said's theory of Orientalism as a lens for cultural depiction means the acknowledgment of biological generalizations, cultural constructions, and racial and religious oversimplifications; it elides all identities of a region into one amorphous mass without finer distinction. Orientalism has often perpetrated racial stereotypes of Asian people; much of this stereotyping is found in the discourse of the "yellow peril," racial characterizations and images used to depict Asian (typically Japanese and Chinese) migrants to the United States in the nineteenth century. The term "yellow peril" lost its specificity and became "a catchword signifying the 'yellow menace' [Asian immigration more generally] to Western Christian civilization."[5] John Dower writes that "the Yellow Peril was naturally the stuff of fantasy and cheap thrills, a fit subject for pulp literature, comics, B-movies, and sensational journalism"; true as that may be, the impact on the lived experiences of Asian migrants to the United States was massive.[6]

Throughout the mid-nineteenth century, Chinese immigration to the United States steadily rose. In 1882 the United States passed the Chinese Exclusion Act, the first immigration policy to target a single country. Naturally, political cartoonists of the day leaped on the opportunity to use all manner of visual stereotypes and tropes to portray Chinese immigrants as soon as the act was announced. One example is Thomas Nast's "The Coming Man," published in the *Wasp* in early 1882. The image plays on the most common fears of the American population:

that Chinese immigrants would take over American society and enterprise. The Coming Man's outstretched hand, complete with talons, is stamped with the word "MONOPOLY"; he is dressed in exaggerated traditional Chinese clothing and wears his hair in a long queue.[7] The image speaks directly to some of the most pressing fears of the time, fanned into flame by magazines such as the *Wasp*, which were known for inflammatory (and often outright racist) content.[8]

"The Coming Man" displays many of the visual tropes that are a staple of anti-Asian images: talons for nails, a queue (usually very long, with a frayed end like a whip), very small or nonvisible eyes, a large nose, and animalistic teeth or saliva protruding from the mouth. The figure is often depicted grabbing or reaching for something, while holding themselves as an animal would. The overall depiction is a less-than-human figure, both animalistic and cruel in one body. Among the most ubiquitous and enduring of the characters that grew from the yellow peril is Dr. Fu Manchu, created by Sax Rohmer in 1912. Fu Manchu embodies many Western fears of Asia: "Asian mastery of Western knowledge and technique (denoted by his degrees from three European universities in chemistry, medicine, and physics); his access to mysterious 'Oriental occult' powers (his eyes can hypnotize victims); and his ability to mobilize the yellow hordes."[9]

Hostility, exclusion, and sociolegal suppression underpinned by Sinophobia continued well into the twentieth century, fueled by this stereotyping. Though hostility toward China declined during World War II, as a result of its stand against Japan, understanding of the differences between Chinese and Japanese immigrants to the United States was limited, and the day-to-day experience of racism was largely unchanged. After World War II, with new allegiances being drawn, the victory of the Chinese Communist Party and Mao Zedong coincided with the beginning of the Cold War; the enemy changed from "yellow" to "red." In this new fight, the "Red Chinese" and their communist allies were deemed to be a threat to U.S. (and, by extension, Western) security. The caricatures of Asian people that had persisted through the yellow peril were reconstructed for this new enemy; these cultural caricatures were staples of representation for a massive amount of Asian ethnic and cultural groups, without nuance, regardless of their actual beliefs and positions.

A 2017 paper by researchers in Japan used several facial analysis methods to ascertain whether Caucasian and Southeast and East Asian people use similar facial expressions for anger, disgust, fear, happiness, sadness, and surprise.[10] The results suggest that there are cultural and physiological differences in the way facial expressions are performed and, furthermore, that cross-cultural recognition of these expressions is not a foregone conclusion. Charles Darwin theorized that "facial expressions are considered as the universal language, recognized across different races and cultures," but this is not the case.[11] Though this is a small issue, it is likely to affect the rendering of faces in comics that depict Southeast Asian characters, especially if the artists are working from photographic reference and are not necessarily able to decode the facial expressions shown.

Of course, there are physiological and anatomical differences in the appearance of Caucasian and Southeast Asian people.[12] It would be unusual to suggest this was not the case, and comics that did so would face a new host of issues relating to race erasure, rather than stereotyping. In terms of facial aesthetics, Caucasian people tend to have "more pronounced three-dimensionality with larger, more deeply set eyes . . . narrower faces and greater vertical height."[13] In contrast, Southeast Asian people "tend to have a wider face with shorter vertical height, which is flat or concave in the medial maxilla [upper jaw] and has a lack of brow, nasal, and chin projection," as well as epicanthal folds on the eyelids.[14] In addition, the average height and weight of a nineteen-year-old Vietnamese man, according to twenty-first-century statistics, is 165.7 centimeters (5 feet 5 inches) and 53.6 kilograms (118 pounds).[15] During periods of war, where food shortages, disease, and stress would be major factors for all, it is highly likely that this basic anatomy would be affected by malnutrition and poor physical health. It is doubtful that the Vietnamese soldiers would match the U.S. troops in physical size, but there are definite advantages to a smaller stature. And it is also unlikely that the height and build difference is as extreme as that shown in figure 1, a panel from *Cheyenne Kid* 58 (1966).[16] If the average Vietnamese man is five feet five, then the blond man (American, we assume) appears to be unusually tall. This is, of course, not a feasible comparison and takes physiological difference to a caricaturish extreme, infantilizing the Vietnamese man. He may never reach the height of his "bigger brother," the American, but the outstretched arm acts as a sort of growth target, or perhaps a taunt.

The anatomical and physiological difference in the way that American and Vietnamese characters are visually created is less rooted in reality than in caricature, racism, and purposeful visual othering. When the physiological differences mentioned above are condensed, as is typical in comics, to a small number of visual signifiers, it is highly likely that they will become stereotyped and, when drawn in "comedic" fashion, become reductionist. The visual tropes for depicting Vietnamese (and other Southeast Asian) people are, as already mentioned, bound up in the long-standing cartooning tropes of the yellow peril and the concept of the enemy image. In terms of war comics, it was not in comics of the Vietnam War that such visuals were first used; such images were widespread during World War II, with special focus on the Japanese.

THE TYPICAL VIET CONG GUERRILLA IS A SCRAWNY, UNKEPT 100-POUNDER WHO BARELY COMES UP TO THE AVERAGE GI'S SHOULDERS UNLIKE THE AMERICAN AND VIETNAMESE SOLDIER, WHO MOST OFTEN MOVE VIA PLASTIC BOAT, JEEP OR HELICOPTER, HE TRAVELS UP TO 40 MILES A DAY ON FABRIC RUBBER-SOLED SHOES.

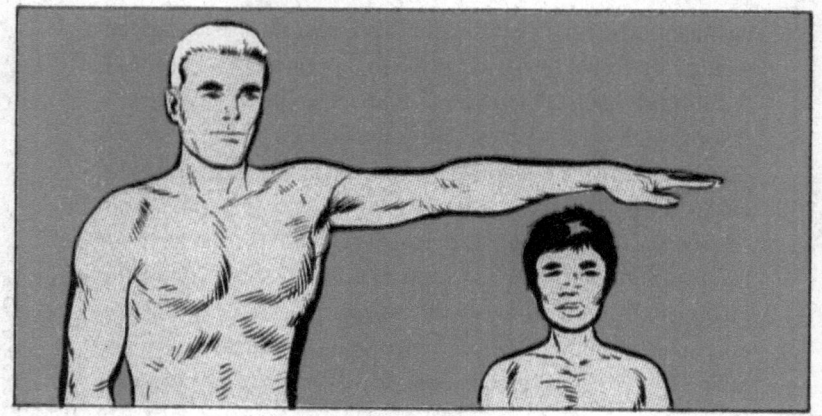

1. The height difference between American and Vietnamese men is exaggerated to strengthen the former and infantilize the latter. *Jungle War Stories* 2, Whitman and Colletta, 1963, p. 36. © Dell Publishing. Image presented under fair use legislation.

Writing about the perception of the Japanese during World War II, Dower suggests that "the visceral hatred of the Japanese tapped Yellow Peril sentiments that, before the turn of the century, had been directed mainly against the Chinese."[17] He goes on to write, "The Japanese, so 'unique' in the rhetoric of World War II, were actually saddled with racial stereotypes that Europeans and Americans had applied to non-whites for centuries: during the conquest of the New World, the slave trade, the Indian wars in the United States, the agitation against Chinese immigrants in America, the colonization of Asia and

Africa, the U.S. conquest of the Philippines at the turn of the century. These were stereotypes, moreover, which had been strongly reinforced by nineteenth century Western science."[18] The U.S. military issued a short comic by Milton Caniff called "How to Spot a Jap," which uses specific visual and physiological stereotypes to differentiate between Chinese and Japanese individuals.[19] It is a bizarre document. For example, Japanese skin tone is described as "lemon yellow," and Japanese people are supposedly identifiable as having a gap between their toes.

Such stereotyping was common across portrayals of the Japanese, who were always shown as villains. Discussing the representation of Japanese and Japanese American characters, Allan Austin and Patrick Hamilton write that "after erasing the differences between both groups and thus positioning Japanese Americans outside of America, comics, cartoons, and movie serials presented both as disloyal, wholly other, dehumanized, violent, and treacherous."[20] The extreme negativity of these characters was largely due to the involvement of the Writers' War Board (WWB), a quasi-governmental domestic propaganda collective that sought to mold popular media in the shape of contemporaneous stereotypes and national allegiances. Indeed, the WWB had tremendous power, considering they were "ostensibly a volunteer organization."[21] Paul Hirsch writes, "The WWB wove propaganda into popular culture to fuel a hatred of fascism, encourage racial tolerance in American society, and promote postwar international cooperation. Beginning in April 1943, the WWB used comic books to shape popular perceptions of race and ethnicity as well as to build support for the American war effort. . . . Board-approved stories initially depicted Japanese and Germans as racially and culturally defective yet also eminently beatable opponents. But as the war dragged on, the WWB requested increasingly brutal depictions of Germans and Japanese as fundamentally, irredeemably evil, and violent."[22] The depictions grew out of yellow peril visual tropes, but they were not rooted in reality. They were copies of copies of copies. Regardless, the same visual tropes endured. After World War II, comics creators continued to design Asian and Asian American villains in line with these tropes. Consider, for example, the Yellow Claw, a caricaturish Communist mandarin, who is hunted by Chinese American FBI agent Jimmy Woo in *Yellow Claw* 1 (1956). Again, we see the use of claws and talons to animalize and dehumanize Asian characters.

The same stereotyping techniques that were used during and following World War II reappear in comics about Vietnam. These stereotypes endure because of their ability to quickly and effectively create the Other, who may or may not be the enemy. Marja Vuorinen writes that "enemy images are the paragon of negative stereotyping."[23] She continues, "As cognitive structures they enable a relevant comparison between categories and make individuals understandable as average members of a group. Even though all stereotypes definitely are not enemy images, all enemy images are stereotypes in the most negative sense of the word."[24] The term itself builds on the concept of the "mirror image," popularized within international relations scholarship. Frank and Melville suggest that, during wartime, the enemy is viewed with only negative characteristics, and such perceptions will flood the media coverage, fueling hatred on both sides. They write, "As the mutual formation of the image of the enemy develops, the adversary is progressively dehumanized. Members of hostile groups see each other as bestial and subhuman on the one hand, and diabolically clever on the other. In either case, this perception seriously weakens inhibitions humans may possess against attacking fellow humans. Destroying vermin or devils becomes a praiseworthy, even holy activity."[25] The creation of the enemy image demands a process of othering, "by which a dominant in-group ('Us,' the Self) constructs one or many dominated out-groups ('Them,' Other) by stigmatizing a difference—real or imagined—presented as a negation of identity and thus a motive for potential discrimination."[26] Everything perceived to be opposite to the ally is negative, evil, and must be destroyed. It does not matter if the image is accurate, so long as it is effective. This is especially relevant in Vietnam, as the United States entered a complex geopolitical struggle. According to David Beard, "to justify a war, the United States needed to project fears outward onto an enemy who had to be eliminated. If friendship brings a people together, enemyship unites them, too, in opposition to someone else, real or imagined."[27]

Vuorinen states, "The image of an enemy is essentially an image of threat."[28] The keyword here is "image." An image does not necessarily have to convey the pure truth of a situation or an individual; in fact, it rarely does. Such images are highly mediated and condensed visual signs that point to specific cultural and political ideals; they are socially formative. The enemy image is about political optics far more than it is about accurate representation. Nick Turse emphasizes the overwhelming lack of understanding that the American troops held when it came to on-the-ground identification of civilians, enemies, and allies: "The plethora of designations and the often-hazy distinctions between them underscore the fact that the Americans never really grasped who the enemy was."[29] Without the clear guidelines of defined battle spaces, or uniforms, there was a large chance of miscataloging friend as foe. And the whole issue was compounded even before troops arrived in-country. Turse recalls a veteran who "told [him] that his training made it clear that the enemy is anything with slant eyes who lives in the village. It doesn't make any difference if it's a woman or child."[30] Soldiers began to speak of the "mere gook rule," also known as the MGR, which "held that all Vietnamese—northern and southern, adults and children, armed enemy and innocent civilian—were little more than animals, who could be killed or abused at will."[31] This mental programming of "gook = enemy" is referenced in *Hellblazer* 5, when one marine references the MGR after killing an elderly Vietnamese man: "He don't look like Charlie. Still, the brass say, if it's yellow and dead—it's an enemy."[32]

During the Vietnam War, the same conflating racist lens that governed military (mis)understanding of the Vietnamese was demonstrated throughout a large swath of comics published both during the war and after. The same kinds of visual tropes for the representation of the Vietnamese are also applied more broadly to people from East Asia, eliding any nuance of North and South Vietnam to instead create a racially and visually ambiguous monoculture.

Here we see the clearest silencing of the Vietnamese people. The subsumption of the country's population into one amorphous mass of "yellow enemies" erases and silences many centuries of cultural development and nuance. The country has a rich history, with the first state considered to be the Hồng Bàng dynasty, established in 2879 BC.[33] Vietnam has been a place of conflict for most of its long history, with frequent invasion and colonization attempts, including the Portuguese in the early 1500s and the French in the mid-1600s. The territory that is known as modern Vietnam was unified in 1792 under the rule of Gia Long.[34] A steady stream of influences that have come into Vietnam since its birth has had a huge effect on the cultural and ethnic composition of the country. And now Vietnam is a highly diverse country with fifty-four recognized ethnic groups (the largest being the Kinh, at around 80 percent of the population) and multiple languages that span seven language groups (Viet-Muong, Tay-Thai, Mong-Dao, Ka-Dai, Tang Mien, Nam Dao, and Han).[35]

The effect of the erasure of Vietnamese history from the conflict is twofold. First, it reduces the Vietnamese people to a singular culture that accurately represents no one. Such simplification and elision of cultural diversity creates a watered-down and ahistorical nothingness that speaks to the lived reality of none of the players. This is tremendously useful for representational purposes as it offers a range of types that can be used by the media and popular culture without effort. Furthermore, as these types are almost certainly negative in their presentation, they are ideal bases for the enemy image. A glib response may be that "no Vietnamese person was consulted in the creation of this picture" and that it is unlikely that anyone would recognize the image as representing them. But those responses are irrelevant; the enemy image needs only to speak to those for whom it is created—in this case, the Americans.

Second, the monoculture of Vietnam, according to the American-constructed enemy image, gives mythmaking control solely to the United States. The war, as mentioned previously, becomes about the United States alone, and they become the active party in a conflict that was not theirs. In the rest of this chapter, I consider how the stereotypes and visual tropes I have just discussed are operationalized in comics of the war, working chronologically and considering not only the representation of the Vietnamese but how the specific tropes at play are relevant to the comics' proximity to the war.

Drawing the Vietnamese during the War

The NLF lurks and lingers at the edges of American characters' interactions and motivations. The enemy are ever present, but their presence is often neither tangible nor visible. The reader knows that they are there—their location is often pinpointed by their gunfire More broadly, with no enemy, there is no war. But they are removed as characters and, therefore, as agents. The character is not so much the Vietnamese but their conspicuous absence. Of course, there is a tremendous benefit to *not* representing the enemy—especially as this is a civil war. If artistic representation is relying on racialized enemies, constructed from stereotypes, then how does the artist construct the ally, who may also be the enemy's brother?[36] Huxley also points out that "the wily oriental officer, so common in the comics of the Second World War and Korea, hardly ever appears in Vietnam stories. A possible explanation for this lies in the nature of the war itself. Vietnam was a major guerrilla war, very different from America's previous wars."[37] This enemy hides; he does not stand up and fight. He is "pushed to the periphery of the comic frame, not even given the dignity of appearing as a wily oriental officer figure. It is as if the presentation of such officers might suggest that the Vietcong had a strategy wider than the continual small-scale ambushes which dominate many comic stories. It is easier to see the enemy as a coward who hides in tunnels and refuses to fight."[38] Here is the first type of erasure and silencing. We do not typically see Vietnamese "brass," though American officers receive much page space. The Vietnamese, in being shown leaderless, become a rabble.

In the introduction, I mentioned that one of the earliest comics stories about the war in Vietnam is "The Raiders' Roost" (1953). There are no Vietnamese characters within the story, per se, except as victims of air strikes; they are shown being killed from above, still clutching their weapons. In one panel, the Vietnamese man being shot looks remarkably like Fidel Castro. However, in general, the enemy (here the Việt Minh) are absent from the narrative, represented only as bursts of gunfire or dying soldiers, and referred to using racist slurs.[39]

Việt Minh characters are absent from "Dien Bien Phu!" published in *Two-Fisted Tales* 40 (1955). The Battle of Điện Biên Phủ was among the most important clashes between French and Vietnamese troops; the victory of the Việt Minh led to the French withdrawal and the division of the country. The French aim had been to cut off supply lines and force the Việt Minh into confrontation, which the French predicted they would win due to their air support and superior weaponry. Under General Giáp, the Việt Minh surrounded and besieged the French, having navigated heavy artillery over difficult terrain. The battle lasted nearly two months, and the failure of French resupply by air left them largely stranded. The victory for Giáp and his soldiers in May 1954 changed the entire conflict. It is undoubtedly one of the most significant Vietnamese victories, but they are absent from their own story. One single panel shows Vietnamese soldiers: two men brandish weapons and shout, "Diệt Pháp" ("Destroy France").[40]

Where are the Vietnamese, and why are they erased from their own conflict? The war was, after all, both a war of independence from colonial powers and a civil war. It is perhaps more confusing that the Việt Minh are missing from *Two-Fisted Tales* because it was an explicitly antiwar publication. The comic's creator, Harvey Kurtzman, was clear that he felt "very strongly about not wanting to say anything glamorous about war, and everything that went before *Two-Fisted Tales* had glamorized war."[41] This story does not glamorize the battle at all, but it does erase an entire perspective and reduce the (victorious) enemy to a single panel. This may be what was necessary to avoid glorification. Instead of a narrative of Vietnamese victory against the odds, it is a story of French hubris. Whatever the logic in the decision, the resulting removal of half of the story is something we see repeatedly, not only in comics of the Vietnam War but in all forms of popular culture. The war serves as a backdrop for stories of American soldiers' bravery and bonding, their valor, camaraderie, and traumata. In most of these comics, the Americans take center stage, and the Vietnamese (regardless of their affiliations or lack thereof) are bit players. Indeed, it is not so much that half the story is missing but that the story that is being told was never meant to include those groups. It is a white, Western narrative solely.

At this juncture, we must view comics within the institutional and publication contexts of their time; this view goes beyond the recognition of outdated racist stereotyping. Rifas suggests that "forces on three levels shape the content of comic books, including war comics."[42] He argues that "profitability is the single most important factor determining the content of American comic books."[43] This means not only that the military was able to influence (or fully suppress) "pacifist comic books, apparently without resistance from the publishers," given that a significant amount of sales were made to military bases, but more broadly that comics narratives were closely directed by the readership.[44] The American readership was used to World War II comics narratives of masculine, military strength and heroism. Vietnam War comics could not ignore their readership and shift focus toward a people who were strangers and a war that was not fully understood. Therefore, for comics to be profitable, they needed to follow characters that Americans both recognized and cared about.

When Vietnamese characters are depicted in earlier war comics, they are typically nonspeaking roles characterized by all the expected visual stereotypes, making them appear malevolent or "exotic" (or both). It is important to remember the timeline of the war at this point. The United States was not engaged in combat until March 8, 1965, with the landing of 3,500 marines near Da Nang; prior to this, the United States was acting in a self-described "advisory" role under the MAAG program. The role of the United States, therefore, is markedly different from that of combatants. It is far easier to argue for helping a group of people (here the United States advising the

South Vietnamese) if *they* are not portrayed as monstrous and *their enemy is*. Consequently, these comics typically show the North Vietnamese as monstrous or as intensely dangerous (e.g., the hidden ambushing assassin), while the South Vietnamese (and apolitical civilians) are largely absent. When the ally is shown, it is often within a village, as a silent, infantilized woman or child. Here, the village represents community and safety. It is a space that is, for the most part, constructed as a place of civilization. The village sits in contrast to the jungle, the wild and untamed space of ambush and booby traps. Broadly speaking, the South are aligned to the village, and the North to the jungle. This will change toward the end of the war and afterward, when the village becomes a contested space and site of both massacre and resistance.

The combat power of the Vietnamese—both North and South—is massively underestimated by the infantilization and feminization that sits at the root of many of these depictions. While the American sits in a vague paternalistic role of the advisor and the ARVN are goofy and useless, the NLF are mostly unseen. This underestimation is referenced by Dower in relation to similar miscalculations regarding the Japanese in World War II. He quotes the civil rights activist Roy Wilkins when he writes: "The disaster at Pearl Harbor was due at least partly to the stupid habit of white people looking down on all non-white nations."[45] Despite the impressive victory at Điện Biên Phủ, these nonwhite combatants receive scant respect as soldiers.

The role of the American military as advisors is the central focus in *Jungle War Stories* (1962–65). During this time, the U.S. intervention is categorized under MAAG, and so the three main characters in this series are all placed in advisory roles within ARVN units. Wright states that "the early issues paralleled the escalation of American involvement in Vietnam and justified U.S. policy there as necessary for the containment of Communism."[46] The title's explicit mention of the jungle sets up the understanding that the majority of the action will be taking place in the jungle, while stories are typically bookended with scenes in the village (a "call to arms" at the beginning and concluding conversations, often with jokes or puns, to close); the divide between jungle and village is clear. It would be fair to assume that in a comic that places American personnel within ARVN units, there would be positive representation of the Vietnamese military. However, this is distinctly not the case. Throughout the series, the ARVN are positioned as weak and cowardly, poorly trained, and childlike in their naivete.

The first issue, "Requiem for a Red," follows Sergeant "Cactus" Kane and his attempts to train a particularly ineffective Vietnamese ranger named Lo Chuong. The rangers have been unable to stand up to NLF aggression, and the civilians of the area are similarly helpless. In one panel, a young woman clutches her baby while screaming, "Where are our defenders?"[47] The story makes clear that the defender, here shown as Lo Chuong, is unable to assist due to cowardice and lack of training. It is for the wisecracking Americans to take the Vietnamese on a crash course in military training and make them into an effective fighting force. The insinuation is insulting, but the stereotyping remains. The North is portrayed as a monstrous, Soviet-supplied enemy of tremendous firepower and remarkable skill. The South, on the other hand, are incompetent without the assistance of the Americans, who appear to act with eye-rolling insouciance: "Observing the dismal state of the South Vietnamese regulars, an American soldier in one story concludes that 'these people got no belly for fighting the Viet Cong guerrillas!'"[48]

Civilians are met with similar disdain for their lack of understanding. In "A Walk in the Sun," the Americans are assigned to relocate a village population to a strategic hamlet. Cactus

Kane states that "half the peasants want no part of it," to which Duke Larsen replies, "There'll always be folks who figure the world owes them a living."[49] Their exchange suggests an unusual understanding of the conflict. Rather than empathizing with the villagers, who have endured massive disruption to their lives, before now being asked to leave their home, the Americans only see their reluctance, interpreting it as laziness, entitlement, and selfishness. This plays into the overarching image of the South Vietnamese as children who need guidance. Here, however, the village leader is converted to the American way of thinking "after seeing the atrocities committed by the Communists and observing the Americans giving medical attention and food to the Vietnamese people."[50] The comic is heavily propagandistic, as if all that is needed to "convert" the Vietnamese is to see that Americans are good for their country and that "the Red dogs" are the true enemy.[51] As much as *Jungle War Stories* appeared to support the United States—and the role of MAAG—it also remains clear in its focus on the ambiguity of enemy and ally. The South Vietnamese can turn in favor of the Americans . . . and they can also turn against. The North, in their stealth and ownership of the jungle, could appear at any time. The lines between friend and foe are not clearly defined. By the late 1960s, it was becoming increasingly likely that the United States was not going to win this conflict, and so characterizations of both South and North Vietnamese had to change. Support for the war was already waning, and so showing the United States losing to a silly collection of monkey-like characters would not be popular. Similarly, depicting the ARVN as childish and naive was unlikely to be popular. The enemy had to become devious and monstrous, while also sneaky and underhanded. The construction of monsters and the assignation of monstrosity are powerful political and discursive tools that can justify or sanction killing the enemy.

More familiar (racist) artistic representational choices are made in *Fightin' Marines* 49 (1962) and 67 (1966), *War Heroes* 17–19 (1966–67), and *Fightin' Five* 35 (1964), which appears to show the NLF as swamp monsters, ambushing American troops from a river. We should pay particular attention to the use of color here. In these full-color comics, the skin tone of the Vietnamese characters varies from subtly different from that of Caucasian American characters to fluorescent yellow.[52] *Tales of Suspense* 39 (1963) features a Vietnamese Communist character named Wong-Chu, who is "menacing" a small village in South Vietnam.[53] Wong-Chu follows all the visual stereotypes we expect of an Asian "villain" and resembles an overweight Fu Manchu. He speaks of himself in the third person, using broken, pidgin English. Wong-Chu is unequivocally the villain of the story, and the otherness of his character is highlighted in the juxtaposition to Professor Yinsen, who is also Southeast Asian but whose representation is slightly less offensive. Visually, Professor Yinsen bears likeness to Ho Chi Minh. Though he is on the "good side" in this comic, Wong-Chu's visual presentation still hints at the enemy—Communism and the NLF. The visual othering—and the use of negative and offensive stereotypes to highlight villainy—is clearly shown in these two characters. These comics are not beholden to visual stereotyping that invokes only the negative, as the multilayering in the portrayal of Yinsen demonstrates. There *is* nuance here, but it is muddied by many layers of caricature and pidgin English.

A similar example of what I might (generously) call "confused nuance" of representation is shown in *Captain America* 125 (1970). While the physical drawings are largely inoffensive, the Vietnamese characters speak in a form of pidgin English that mimics how English-speaking writers might imagine that nonnative English speakers may sound.[54] We may also consider *Cheyenne Kid* 58 (1966) in a similar vein. The story "The Happy

Hunting Ground" likens the NLF to "the finest guerrilla fighters the world has ever known . . . the Apaches, Sioux, Kiowa, Comanche, and the Cheyenne."⁵⁵ Considering the position of Indigenous Americans within the general canon of American history and culture, this comparison is not necessarily a compliment. The short comic draws parallels between Indigenous American (here called "Indian") soldiers and the NLF (here the "Viet Cong"). The comic recounts several NLF traits but then one-ups them. The NLF is patient and able to remain hidden, but Indigenous American soldiers do it better!⁵⁶ The Indigenous American is clearly coded as such by "displaying key signature items" of costume, as Chad Barbour notes: "the buckskins, headbands, moccasins, feathers, and warpaint accoutrements by which the white Indian comics character creates the visual effect of his heroic persona."⁵⁷ As such, the heroism that may be associated with Indigenous Americans is co-opted to become generally American and, furthermore, white American.

Visually, neither the Indigenous American characters nor the NLF are offensively represented (though the NLF are inexplicably shirtless). All written information in the comic is conveyed via caption boxes; no character speaks. Though the images are largely uncontroversial, the links made between the Indigenous Americans and NLF within the caption boxes are problematic. The captions highlight the sense of otherness between white Americans and both the NLF and the Indigenous Americans. For example, the comic closes with the words "Just as they did in World War II, Korea, and other places, the American Indian in Vietnam is proving himself to be still one of the finest fighting men the world has ever known."⁵⁸ Besides raising the question of "proving himself to whom?" there is a definite disconnect evident in the description posed here. The "American Indian" is held as distinct and separate from the "American." It is important to note here that though the U.S. Army was racially segregated until the signing of Executive Order 9981 in 1948, this did not include Indigenous Americans, who mostly served in non-segregated units. The consideration of Indigenous American soldiers as being in some way separate to "American" soldiers is therefore not a feature of the structure of the military itself but a cultural and social distinction. The NLF are similar, though not equal or superior, to Indigenous American soldiers, who are an important, though separate, part of the U.S. military.

Toward the end of the 1960s, as both the war and the antiwar movement were gaining in momentum and media coverage, Vietnamese characters began to feature more prominently on the cover of comics. Two especially striking examples of racist stereotyping and a bold, ill-advised choice of color were published in 1967. The cover of *Our Fighting Forces* 105 shows Captain Hunter fighting with an NLF soldier.[59] The soldier is holding a bright-red grenade to Hunter's face; Hunter pulls away and grasps his enemy by the wrist. Both faces are contorted. Hunter wears the typical olive uniform, while the NLF soldier wears black *áo bà ba* and a *nón lá*.[60] On first look, the red grenade looks like a human heart, heightening the implied savagery of the NLF. However, what is most striking is the color difference in skin. Hunter grabs the Vietnamese man's wrist, and we see the clear distinction of skin tones. Hunter is represented in typical Caucasian skin tone, whereas his adversary is an alarming shade of orange yellow. His face is similarly marked with the expected visual stereotyping, especially around the eyes and teeth.

The second example comes from *Super Green Beret* 1 (1967), created by the short-lived publisher Lightning Comics.[61] Figure 2 shows the first cover of this series. The main character, Tod Holton, is holding an NLF soldier by the neck while hitting another in the face. A final character, in PAVN uniform, is hit on the head. The three Vietnamese faces are grotesque in both

2. Tod Holton fights three Vietnamese soldiers with apparent ease. *Super Green Beret* 1, Pfeufer and Marston, 1967. © Lightning. Image presented under fair use legislation.

features and coloration: all three men have simian features. There is a definite animal quality to the faces that highlights a clear disconnect between the handsome, Caucasian Tod Holton and the animalistic Vietnamese.

As with the cover of *Our Fighting Forces*, the two figures are grabbing each other, presenting an opportunity for close comparison of the skin tones of both characters. Holton is pale pink, which looks appropriate for a white character, whereas the Vietnamese characters are an intense shade of mustard yellow. The simian features and yellow skin may not have been so striking if it were not for the presence of Holton. Holton's face is clear and unblemished. He is smiling, and his face shows no mark of effort, which is unusual, given that he is fighting three men. This implies that the American is unmarked by warfare and will emerge unscathed. His face, though stereotypically handsome, has little detail. He is strongly built, but his features are basic. This is a face onto which you could project any identity. When placed against his adversaries, the distinction is clear—the strong, white American will easily crush the monstrous and grotesque Vietnamese. This is the enemy image at work: ugliness and animalism as the opposite of clean-cut, all-American white masculinity.

The stark difference in facial features and the bold choice in coloration of these cover images serve two purposes. First, they highlight the sense of otherness between the two sides of the comic, though the cover does not make it clear who the enemy is—are they NLF, PAVN, or even ARVN? But it does not matter. The enemy is Vietnamese, and their physical depiction makes this clear. Furthermore, it conflates Vietnamese and "yellow," which harkens back to the yellow peril imagery. It conflates Vietnamese with monkeys, which reduces the enemy to the status of mere beasts, a common tactic for diminishing their abilities. The enemy, and furthermore the enemy image, is as far from the perfect American dream as we can imagine. Second, it clearly shows the audience what this comic *is*. In 1967 the newsstands were bursting with many different genres and titles. The covers of both *Our Fighting Forces* 105 and *Super Green Beret* 1 show what these comics are doing (i.e., they are, primarily, war comics, following the tropes that readers would expect) and how they are doing it (i.e., the American Green Berets are kicking ass in Vietnam). There is no ambiguity here. The comic clearly tells the reader to expect a Manichean war story in which the United States and Vietnam fight, but the United States easily wins. In these comics covers, we see the U.S. narrative of the Vietnam War played out: "The Vietnamese are plucky and will try to win, but we will prevail."

At this point, it is important to remember that comic books are physical items; during this period, they were printed as quickly and cheaply as possible. These creative parameters are going to affect the finished object, and it is highly likely that the printing technology available will not be able to capture the visual nuance that is needed for the representation of a wide range of skin tones. From the 1890s, color comics had been printed with benday dots, a technique that uses four-color printing dots that are closely spaced, widely spaced, or overlapping, depending on the effect and color needed. The process made it possible to create inexpensive brightly colored shading, as well as "secondary colors such as green, purple, orange, and flesh tones."[62] However, a more limited palette made sense to cut costs and to avoid having to pay union rates to skilled engravers.

Guy Lawley makes the point that, while pure yellow faces are "genuinely puzzling," it is likely that the printers are attempting to "render some kind of orangey tint which was perhaps more within the range of actual healthy human existence ... at least, given the essentially diagrammatic nature of much comic book art."⁶³ The CMYK printing system had only three possible values: nominally 25 percent, 50 percent, and 100 percent (in practice, these values varied widely). The full color range included only sixty-three colors (sixty-five including black and white). Prior to 1969, DC Comics did not use 25 percent or 50 percent yellow tints. DC's Caucasian characters were R2; Indigenous Americans were R3. Marvel's Caucasians people were Y2R2 (meaning that 25 percent yellow had been added to pale pink). There is scant research on the use of printing in the (re)creation of skin tones in comics, but the small amount of evidence available suggests that, at best, nuance and cultural sensitivity were not an issue. At worst, such issues were actively ignored as irrelevant.⁶⁴ While none of this excuses the use of other racist tropes (facial features and pidgin English), it does go some way to suggest that the use of more jaundiced shades of yellow is not solely due to racism—but the ultimate acceptability of those shades and tones might still be.

Tables Turning: Comics after the War

Jungle War Stories is the longest continuous comics run published during the period of the war that included narratives of the conflict.⁶⁵ Likewise, only one film was released during the period: *The Green Berets*, starring John Wayne (1968). The reasons for this pop-culture reticence are myriad, with most relating to the profitability of a series and the readership's desire for characters and narratives that they can relate to. The two substantial comics series that were specifically about the war were not published until the mid-1980s. This means that series with the opportunity to develop arcs and narrative-trope continuity appeared in a period characterized by the recognition of trauma and the need for healing and reconciliation. It is understood that this is going to affect representation of the enemy, though this is, of course, not consistent. And for the most part, the same overarching issues that we find in earlier stories are still at play here.

Hints at the conflict and its effects appear in many titles that are not war comics, likely to give a sense of time and dimension to the story world of the 1960s and 1970s. These stories focus on American troops and camaraderie, the relationship between the men, or the aftermath of their tours and their long, grueling recovery. In titles including *Sgt. Rock* 311 and 354 (1977), *The Human Fly* 15 (1978), *Marvel Team-Up* 118 (1982), *GI Joe* 42 (1985), *Scout* 14 (1986), *Hellblazer* 5 (1988), and *Cinder and Ashe* (1988), the only presence that any Vietnamese character has is as a pair of eyes watching in the jungle, perhaps a shadow, and a burst of gunfire. Even multi-issue miniseries, such as *In-Country Nam* (1986) and *Tempus Fugitive* (1990–91) do not take the opportunity to develop any kind of meaningful arc for any non-American characters.

Vietnam does not feature *more* in these comics than in the war period; toward the middle of the 1990s, interest dies off almost completely. However, it was in this period that two of the most well-known (and critically acclaimed) series were published: *The 'Nam* (1986–92) and *Vietnam Journal* (1987–91), both of which I have introduced previously. Though much praise has been laid on *The 'Nam* for its portrayal of the grunts' experience, the narrative space and attention given to Vietnamese characters is astoundingly poor. Across eighty-four issues of the series, there are only six named Vietnamese characters; none of them appear in more than one issue. All six are known only by a single first name and do not have full family names at all; their histories and personal stories are erased. The limited engagement with Vietnamese characters means that there is no opportunity to develop relationships between the U.S.

characters and their Vietnamese counterparts, nor does it allow for a nuanced understanding of the war beyond what the U.S. soldiers may believe is going on.

There is one single issue that gives voice to a Vietnamese character—*The 'Nam 7*, "Good Old Days." In this issue, Private Ed Marks asks Duong, a Kit Carson scout, to explain why he defected from the NLF. Duong begins his story in 1940, with the Japanese invasion and the execution of his wife for her political beliefs; he states that "when they killed her, something within me changed. I was no longer a simple farmer."[66] Duong explains that, after graduating from university and joining the Việt Minh, he went back to his farm, remarried, and allowed himself to "become not political."[67] As the French colonial presence escalates, Duong reenters the military, his second wife is also killed, and he throws himself into fighting for his country. He becomes disenchanted with the ideology of the NLF and defects, positioning the NLF as the "villain" of the story and suggesting that both their methods and their motivations were flawed. In comparison, the Americans are depicted as the benevolent force: "You Americans wanted to help. While my people . . . I do not know what my people were trying to do!"[68] Throughout the entire flashback, there is only one speech bubble, in which a French soldier calls Duong's wife a "subhuman pig"; no Vietnamese character is granted speech.[69] The story closes with a lackluster apology from Marks, though it is not clear if he is apologizing to Duong for asking the question in the first place or for his difficult past.

Two elements of this issue are noteworthy in relation to representational strategies for Vietnamese characters: the statement of historical accuracy and the difference in physical drawings throughout. The issue opens with a written statement from Doug Murray. He writes, "The elements of this story are completely true. Duong's story is actually a composite of the stories of three different VC—not all of whom changed sides and became Kit Carson scouts. By using these stories, I think we've given a clear picture of the roots of the war—the reason Charlie fought as long and hard as he did."[70] The insistence on historical accuracy is not necessarily alien to *The 'Nam*, as I have discussed in the introduction. What is particularly jarring is that this is the only time that the comic provides such statements to lay claim to historical accuracy. This is not a comic that strives to tell "the truth" of the matter, though the vast majority of events shown are generally accurate. This note does not fit with the overall feel of the comic; though we may be tempted to applaud the commitment to research and accuracy here, it also begs the question of why other sections do not deserve similar treatment.

The other issue here is, once again, the visual and artistic choices at play. For the most part, Duong is drawn accurately and without caricature or stereotypical features and skin tone. The flashback story is nuanced, and the motivations of the characters, especially Duong, make sense in relation to the events. At no point is the struggle of the Vietnamese farmers diminished. However, in the scenes that bookend the flashback, he is shown as a purple-faced, wizened, simian man of extremely diminutive build. This is not in line with the drawings of him as a young man. Figures 3 and 4 show a comparison of the two "faces" of Duong. The shriveled man visually undercuts the historically sensitive representations presented in the rest of the issue. The flashback art style and nuance are unusual in relation to the rest of the series, which is highly jarring. Rather than highlighting the different viewpoint of Duong, the story arc is absorbed without comment into the overarching ethos of the series. At no point does Duong's story receive further attention, even in the discussions of American characters. However, though his story is a short interlude to the "regularly

3. & 4. Duong is presented with two different faces: in his own recollections and, later, after he defects. *The 'Nam* 7, Murray, Golden, and Vansant, 1987. © Marvel. Image presented under fair use legislation.

scheduled programming" of the series, it is carefully constructed and historically rigorous.

According to Richard Young, *The 'Nam* is strongly conservative in its ideology. He writes that it "reflected an interpretation of the war which scholars commonly refer to as the 'noble cause.' Popularized by Ronald Reagan during his 1980 election campaign, 'noble cause' rhetoric promoted a revival of nationalist pride about the United States' intervention."[71] By this reckoning, it would make sense that the Vietnamese remain in the background, if they are present at all. It is difficult to stir up nationalist pride while maintaining a nuanced representation of a racial, political, and national Other. In fact, the designation of Vietnamese characters as missing or monstrous has not changed particularly since the 1950s. Though the focus of the stories themselves has developed beyond the gung ho camaraderie of *Jungle War Stories*, and often follows the traumatic experiences and recovery of the soldiers, this focus is squarely on Americans; the Vietnamese are erased again. Before I move to comics published after 2001, there is one final representational issue to consider.

In Mike Grell's *Jon Sable, Freelance*, the titular character served in Vietnam (as a clerk typist in the U.S. Army—a "rear echelon motherfucker," or "REMF") before becoming a mercenary who travels the world getting involved in unusual situations. Though his tour is mentioned in several issues (in off-hand comments and vague, undefined ways), only two issues engage with Vietnam and the war in a substantial manner. In issues 12 and 13, collectively referred to as "M.I.A.," Sable travels to Vietnam with two other veterans to attempt to uncover evidence of prisoners of war still being held and to find a missing pilot. During their time in-country, Sable is attacked by a charging water buffalo, captured by the Vietnamese military, and tortured; any political or geographic allegiances of the military are not made clear in the comic. Again, we return to the ambiguous racial monoculture.

But this comic has an extra dimension to its characterization that is uncommon in these texts; we are introduced to a character who can be seen as a proxy for a historical figure. The creation of comics characters from real-life figures during World War II is relatively common. In all manner of narrative media, the average consumer would be used to seeing (in)famous Nazi leaders and politicians within the story. There are very few names of Vietnamese leaders that have entered popular culture in a comparable way.[72] In *Jon Sable, Freelance* 12 and 13, one of the three who take part in the rescue mission is a former ARVN colonel, Nguyen Van Tran. There is little remarkable about his physical portrayal, besides being noticeably shorter than the American characters. He is working as a dishwasher; when asked if he is willing to "risk all," he replies, "Willing to risk my share of the American dream and a promising career as a dishwasher . . . for a chance to strike one more blow against my enemies—not to mention the twenty-five thousand dollars?"[73] Tran's remark pokes fun at the concept of the American dream. The packaging of American society and culture as a place of freedom and wealth was prevalent throughout the war and endures to this day. However, it is not a clear division of "the USA as paradise vs Vietnam as hell."[74] Rather, as one Vietnamese migrant worker stated in a 2017 interview, "When you think about it and compare America and Vietnam, it is a lonely paradise and happy hell."[75] Economically, the United States might be a safer and more comfortable place to live, but the loss of culture and family ties leads to extreme loneliness and detachment. For Tran, though he is economically safe in the United States, the opportunity to return to his native country and fight is too tempting to pass up. The addition of twenty-five thousand dollars is a welcome extra.

The suggestion that a once successful and respected military colonel could be working at the level of dishwasher is a potentially damning indictment of the American dream and its obvious failure for a substantial number of immigrants and displaced persons. However, Tran's story has much in common with that of Major General Nguyễn Ngọc Loan, who is most famous for his presence in Eddie Adams's award-winning photograph *Saigon Execution*. In February 1968, during the Tet Offensive, Loan shot and killed an NLF member, Nguyễn Văn Lém, in the street in Saigon. The photograph became one of the most enduring of the war, being read as an image of South Vietnamese brutality, the breakdown of the rules of engagement, or the sheer lawlessness of the events in Vietnam on both sides. Loan left Vietnam during the fall of Saigon and settled in Virginia, where he opened a pizzeria.[76] Tran's position is similar to Loan's, as is his attitude toward the United States. Both were forced to move because of the war's conclusion and their actions during it; the United States is a refuge of sorts. But their refuge is not necessarily a place of safety or happiness, more of necessity. Of course, Tran is not a full rendering of Loan within *Jon Sable, Freelance*. He is a character made in Loan's mold, to show what could—and did—happen to high-ranking Vietnamese officers. The hint at Loan's story highlights the lack of "true life characters" that feature in these comics and the overall dearth of historical Vietnamese characters within popular culture.

From the late seventies to the late nineties, Asian enemies and villains in popular culture were commonplace. The enemy's face was typically Communist, following Cold War allegiances and anxieties, and oftentimes this meant East and Southeast Asian (as opposed to Soviet or Eastern European). However, the attacks of September 11, 2001, brought about a quick and decisive shift in the "default villain."

The Enemy Changes: Representation since 9/11

In Vietnam the enemy was ill-defined and vague. Allies and enemies did not look distinctly different, and uniforms were not a given. However, the threat was not on home soil; it was geographically bound by the theater of conflict. After the events of September 11, 2001, the threat of attack from "within" became more visceral. Furthermore, the enemy was no longer Southeast Asian or Communist. The enemy became Arabs and Muslims. As with the image of the Southeast Asian constructed during the late nineteenth century and the yellow peril, the "Arab is an ethnic icon manufactured painstakingly in the United States since the nineteenth century, an icon that was expedited into political eminence after 9/11."[77] It has been suggested that the "new post-9/11 paradigm" bears several issues that are specific to this event and time: "One problem is the nature of the threat—an 'unspecified enemy.' . . . After 9/11, the American people are undoubtedly aware that there are enemies in their midst, but just who they are, no-one knows."[78] For Kakihari, this vagueness of the enemy—and potentiality for an enemy presence "in their midst"—explains the necessity for clarifying the enemy, as evidenced by statements like the "axis of evil."[79] Though I have demonstrated that the enemy was not a clearly defined concept in Vietnam, the situation is different here.

The image of the enemy as an unknown entity makes Vietnam a useful proxy for the War on Terror. The difference in landscape, types of warfare, racial profiles of the opposing sides, and geopolitical background of the conflict means that Vietnam is not being grafted onto narratives of the wars in Iraq and Afghanistan without some considerable reframing. What is being used instead is the heavy focus on troop relationships and camaraderie, trauma and the mental labor of combat, and the position of Americans in "alien terrain." It is not, therefore,

Vietnam itself that is being used in many of these comics but rather the concept of the conflict as proxy for the current geopolitical and military circumstances.

Vietnam has become a useful touchstone as a backstory for superheroes or other characters. Both Nick Fury and Logan (aka Wolverine, from the X-Men franchise) have appeared in Vietnam, though neither in typical soldier roles; they are parachuted in (sometimes literally) to solve a single issue and then moved back to the United States without engaging with any other part of the conflict at all. For example, in *Web of Venom: Ve'nam* (2018), Fury and Logan are placed in Vietnam to investigate the deaths of a platoon of American soldiers, who have been torn apart. They discover that an eldritch symbiote has been taking over soldiers as a parasite and wreaking havoc. In *Fury: My War Gone By* (2012) Nick Fury makes two trips to Vietnam (not tours, as he is not a typical soldier), again being figuratively parachuted in and working closely with the CIA. The plotlines are complex and involve a considerable amount of political discussion, beyond what we have previously seen in titles such as *The 'Nam* or *Jungle War Stories*. Here, Fury works with a politician, McCuskey, to provide intelligence regarding the American advisory role and to make suggestions regarding U.S. intervention. In both of these comics, the Vietnamese are entirely absent. The landscape of Vietnam—and its political history—becomes a useful background for these characters, but the enemy (and even the ally) do not feature. Again, they are removed from their own story and denied both agency and voice.

The most famous character in this respect is the Punisher (Frank Castle), who has been retconned with a Vietnam vet backstory, since his inclusion in special arcs of *The 'Nam* in 1988 and 1992; these are further examples of parachuting in the hero to deal with a singular issue. Castle features in several Vietnam stories published since 2001, which explicitly position him as a soldier serving his tours in particularly dangerous parts of Vietnam and in suboptimal conditions. His Vietnam origin story is told over two miniseries: *The Punisher: Born* (2011) and *Punisher: The Platoon* (2017).[80] The two series follow his command, beginning in *The Platoon*, as he heads up a platoon based near Khe Sanh. He freely admits to having zero combat experience and asks for the troops to "show [him] the ropes."[81] This story runs parallel to that of Ly Quang, a highly trained NLF soldier who sets her sights on hunting and eradicating "black rifles" (a nickname for Americans, based on the black color of the M16 rifle) after the death of her family at the hands of U.S. soldiers.[82] The story becomes a battle between Castle and Ly, as she disobeys orders to cease, pushing on with what seemingly becomes a private crusade, before being killed in hand-to-hand combat with Castle.

In *The Punisher: Born* the reader follows the narrator, Stevie Goodwin, as he serves under Castle. Having gained combat experience and becoming seriously psychologically affected by the events he witnesses in Vietnam, Castle is sent to Firebase Valley Forge, an outpost that is long forgotten, poorly equipped, and staffed by largely incompetent personnel.[83] Castle becomes increasingly unstable; as his platoon descends into chaos at the overlooked base, he murders a soldier who has previously raped a captured NLF soldier. The base is attacked by the NLF, and in a moment that is either supernatural or a sign of his deteriorating mental health, Castle gives in to the voice in his head. By the end of the series, the attack is passed and most of the characters are dead. Only the mentally destroyed Castle remains.

Both *The Punisher: Born* and *Punisher: The Platoon* use framing devices. In *Born* it is the character of Stevie Goodwin, who acts as narrator and whose voice we hear throughout as the story's guide. In contrast, *The Platoon* has two outer frames. Most of the narrative is told as a flashback, recalled during an interview between an author, Michael Goodwin (brother of Stevie), and four veterans who served under Castle. This is the first frame. The second is another interview, this time between Goodwin and Colonel Letrong Giap, formerly of the PAVN. Both interviews provide half of the story, which comes together through the interviewer-narrator of Goodwin. This particular choice of framing allows for a balanced retelling of the story. Rather than privilege one narrative over the other, the two sets of veterans—previously positioned as enemies—are placed in dialogue. Furthermore, there is no marked shift in artistic style, paneling, or coloration in the two narratives: Frank's and Ly's stories are both displayed in wide bandeau panels and realistic coloration.[84] There is no visual privileging of one narrative over the other either. When the two stories converge in hand-to-hand combat, neither character is prioritized until the fight is won by Castle. I discuss Ly's characterization further in chapter 2.

There is little caricaturing of facial features or physical stature in either comic. All characters, of either nationality, are drawn as realistically as the comics form allows in terms of facial aesthetics and coloration—there is minimal difference in the skin tones of Caucasian and Asian characters. Their identity and side in the conflict are shown via their uniform. However, though the discussion here suggests that the representational strategies in use allow for a nuanced image of the Vietnamese and a balanced focus on both sides of the conflict, this is not strictly true. Where there are Vietnamese characters, they are depicted fairly, but there are not many. For the most part, NLF and PAVN characters are either missing from the action or presented as screaming, dying combatants with no voice or narrative agency. *The Platoon* is forthcoming in showing the other side of the conflict and presents a soldier who is given tremendous respect and power by her fellow North Vietnamese (and by Castle to an extent). *Born* features one Vietnamese character, but she is silent, raped, and then shot. It becomes clear that, for the most part, these comics of the Vietnam War have very little interest in the Vietnamese. It is the Americans' war, and the Vietnamese are only bit players.

Despite their limited number of Vietnamese characters, Garth Ennis's Punisher comics show that there is no need to perpetuate racist visual stereotyping to ensure readability in Vietnam War comics. But the deeply offensive tropes that are commonplace in earlier comics have not died off. There are many examples of post-2001 comics that subscribe to a similar visual ethos and rely on visual tropes that hearken back to the images I have discussed previously. In *Scalped* (2007–12), there are flashback scenes to Vietnam in which the Vietnamese characters are rendered with pronounced buck teeth and exaggerated epicanthal eyelids. In *Guerillas* (2009–16), the enemy are literal gorillas, and it is not clear which side of the conflict they are on. This comic takes the "enemy as simian" to the extreme, literalizing them as fully grown and incredibly dangerous adult gorillas. The final recent example that speaks to the persistence of these tropes within comics about the war is *The Cape 1969* (2012). This is the prequel comic to *The Cape* (2007), which gives the history of the main character's magical cape, which is embroidered with his father's section patch from his tour in Vietnam. Captain Cory Chase served as a medevac pilot in 1969 and was captured by the NLF after a helicopter crash. He is thrown into a cage with an unusual figure—a wizened, heavily tattooed man who appears not to speak any language but can harness magic (see figure 5). Chase is tied to the strange man, and they are forced to fight to the death in a rice paddy.[85] Chase beats the man viciously and holds him underwater until he

5. A wizened Vietnamese man displays tattoos from other nations in a poorly researched pastiche of imagery. *The Cape 1969*, Hill and Ciaramella, 2013. © IDW. Image presented under fair use legislation.

dies. The man's ability to fly is passed to Chase, and Chase uses it to escape and destroy the village in which he was held.

The storyline is standard supernatural horror fodder, albeit incredibly violent in its presentation. The reason I consider it here is the presentation of the antagonist characters. The strange man, as I have been calling him, is a small, hunched, naked, brown man with prominent black tattoos. Tattooing is a widespread practice around the world and forms a key aspect of identity expression for many cultures. However, these tattoos are distinctly *not* a part of Vietnamese culture. The bands and fan shapes are reminiscent of Māori or Pacific Islander traditions, while the fish scale pattern is similar to Japanese Irezumi designs.[86] This character is definitely presented as Other, but there is nothing to suggest that he is Vietnamese.

The result is a caricature of Southeast Asian otherness that conflates a number of different body-art traditions in an attempt to heighten the supernatural aura and "exotic" appearance. The only goal is to create a weird and witchy character; there is no attempt at accuracy. To bring the analysis full circle and return to the original suggestion that Vietnamese characters fill one of two categories, we can say that this character fits in both. The presentation is clearly monstrous, and the inclusion of unexplained magic, paired with his creepy smile, adds to this effect. He is also missing—not visually but verbally. The only words spoken are "Boom Boom," at several points, but there is no explanation of what this means. The character is silenced, stripped of voice and agency, as with so many other Vietnamese characters.

To close, I turn to *The Other Side* (2006–7), by Jason Aaron and Cameron Stewart. This comic shows both sides in the Vietnam War. They are not positioned as explicit enemies, with clear enemy-image stereotypes at play. Rather, Aaron and Stewart put the U.S. Marine Corps and PAVN in direct dialogue to create a story of contrasts and juxtapositions. Originally presented as a five-issue miniseries published by DC, the narrative follows the dual stories of Private Bill Everette, who is drafted into the marines at nineteen, and Vo Binh Dai, also nineteen, who volunteers to join the PAVN; he is the only member of his village to do so. The narrative was inspired by Aaron's cousin, author and Vietnam veteran Gustav Hasford, most famous for his novel *The Short-Timers*.[87] Inspired by his cousin's experiences and subsequent conversations with the First Marine Division 1so Snuffies, Aaron wrote the comic to "center the story on the ground—on a couple of grunts, caught up in a very ugly conflict"; he adds that "*The Other Side* will be the first fullfledged Vietnam War book that DC has published since 1967."[88]

The visual depictions are consistent in their realism across characters of all nationalities. Some facial expressions are presented as monstrous and caricaturish, but this is based on individual characters, not race. For example, the excessively brutal and theatrical drill sergeant has red eyes and a grayish skin tone. Meanwhile, the PAVN guide through the jungle is a heavily scarred young woman whose face is shown only in an angry scowl and lit by candlelight, in a style reminiscent of fireside horror stories, while she recounts her personal traumata at the hands of American soldiers.[89] The drill sergeant's gray face contrasts with the paleness of his recruits, just as the red flame-lit face of the guide is juxtaposed with the muted coloration of the soldiers. The bold use of contrasting color to signify clear differences in character and personality suggests not only that the title—"the other side"—relates to the focus on the opposing side but that the lines of division will not be drawn in the places that we may expect.

This comic is about the two sides of the conflict, but this is not the primary focus. Everette and Dai receive equal page space, their experiences mirror each other, and both are treated with respect in their visual depictions. Both men are side by side to show that there is minor difference in either side. There is little construction of the enemy here, or of an enemy image. Enemies are constructed against the protagonist combatants. Here, both sides are presented together, and though they may be on either side of the conflict, neither is strictly the enemy image.

Rather, the two men begin at opposite ends of the scale, and they quickly become similar. And at the climax of the narrative, the two men are indistinguishable. Their actions follow basic human instinct. The other side is not the United States–North Vietnam split but the different states the characters move through as they experience the war. This is not a comic that places each side in conflict, but rather they are in dialogue, emphasizing their common humanity and the ways in which all humans will resort to certain behaviors at a time of extreme trauma and threat to life. By presenting these characters as sharing the same common humanity, the writers aren't expressing some given prelinguistic and presocial human nature that simply *is*. Recourse to the human as a universal often tends to dehistoricize and depoliticize—a Vietnamese and a U.S. soldier are, for historical, social, and political reasons, different. They are playing by different rules or perhaps entirely different games, as we see in the presentation of Everette's and Dai's motivations for their involvement. When receiving his draft letter, Everette responds, "Fuck me," before attempting to be released from the obligation by telling "their doctor [he] was queer as all get-out and would fuck every boy's ass [he] could get [his] hands on."[90] Everette does not know where Vietnam is.

Dai, on the other hand, stands up to the call. When hearing a soldier using a loud-hailer shout, "Who here is willing to fight and die for the glory of the revolution?" Dai responds without hesitation, "I am."[91] The accompanying panel shows him marching defiantly forward with a determined expression. It is not that Everette is a coward and Dai brave. The conflict means two completely different things to each of them. One man has no history or knowledge of the place and is doing what he is told to do by law and the U.S. government; the other is joining a centuries-long fight for his homeland, with a set of beliefs that are central to his upbringing and identity. They are two totally different stories, brought together through the grim reality of warfare and, furthermore, the fact that this reality affects both sides. No player is dealt an easy hand; the suffering is universal, although experienced in very different ways.

2
From Round-Eye to Sniper Spy

Where Are the Women?

> Giặc đến nhà, đàn bà cũng đánh [When war comes, even women must fight].
>
> —VIETNAMESE SAYING

As Nancy Sinatra's "These Boots Are Made for Walkin'" (1966) plays in the background, a young woman walks toward two men sitting on a street corner. She approaches them, Americans in fatigues, holding her hair above her head and speaking in broken English: "Me so horny! Me love you long time! Me sucky sucky!"[1] The men mock her and pretend to barter for her services and she responds in earnest. This scene is the viewer's introduction to Vietnam in Stanley Kubrick's film *Full Metal Jacket* (1987). The juxtaposition of the men's easy joking and relaxed posture with the woman's awkward sexual affectations and clumsy dirty talk highlights the power imbalance between the two groups: white American men versus Vietnamese women. Though the scene is barely two minutes long and the female character is unnamed, listed in the credits as "Da Nang Prostitute," these lines are among the most iconic in American cinema of Vietnam.[2] But beyond their cinematic legacy, these phrases have become cultural touchstones for both the representation of Asian women in American media and their wider sexualization. Viet Thanh Nguyen writes, "Ever since Puccini's 1904 opera *Madame Butterfly*, which inspired the hit 1989 musical *Miss Saigon*, Asians have been portrayed in romantic terms as self-sacrificing women who prefer white men to Asian men, and who willingly die for the love of white men."[3] This romanticization is a thin veneer that barely conceals the overt sexualization and commodification of Southeast Asian women by Western men; it provides a vague justification for the sexual colonialism that is forced upon them. Vietnamese women are cast as destroyers of men. They are the sex workers who destroy "good American morals," spread disease, and lead men into dangerous situations. Alternatively, they are spies and combatants, far more vicious and devious than their male counterparts. Occasionally, they are voiceless mothers, screaming and running from an aerial attack. In most stories, female Vietnamese characters are portrayed negatively, without nuance or agency, as we have previously seen with Vietnamese characters, in general, in chapter 1.

The other side of this representational coin is the relative veneration of (white) American women, as I demonstrate in this chapter. American women are often cast in the role of a girl next door, which becomes "the symbol of ideal American womanhood—wholesome, a pal rather than a paramour, a mother or a sister rather than a pin-up girl."[4] The girl next door was "part of the 'psychological warfare' of Vietnam," as she not only reminded American men "what they were fighting for" but also represented the "pure ideal," in contrast to the "corrupted" Vietnamese.[5]

American women are positioned as nurturers of men.[6] Within a military setting, they are typically nurses and caregivers, nonsexual and motherly. Those who are presented as commodities—as troop entertainment flown in from the United States—are both sexualized and desexualized. They are presented to titillate, to provide a fantasy vision of "what we are fighting for," but there is a simultaneous desexualization. Whereas Vietnamese women are sexually available, whether consensually or by force, American women are not. They are sexy but not sexual, an attractive object to look at but never to touch.

The history of women as players in major conflicts is a complicated one. Here I offer only a drastic distillation of many centuries of war experience, as it is not my aim to provide a comprehensive study of this topic; rather, I am concerned with how comics address this subject.[7] That said, I wish to make clear that the distinction between battlefield and home is rarely clear and that the role of camp follower has existed for centuries. Most camp followers were wives of soldiers, whose role was to provide (unpaid) domestic labor.[8] Camp followers took up the work that was not provided by the military, as well as support and sexual services. Sex work was a common occurrence; in many places, it was a roaring business. But sex work was only a small portion of the work that was expected of camp followers, be they wives or "rent-a-wives." In the military, as in life, women's domestic roles are erased from the official picture of the world and remain an unacknowledged duty.

Within the United States, women have typically been employed in secretarial, support, and care-giving positions; the role of women in active combat remains controversial. Since the 1970s, most Western armies have begun to enlist women for active duty in all branches. The U.S. military has been accepting female recruits since 1917, with the eventual passing of the Women's Armed Services Integration Act in 1948. By the Vietnam War in the 1960s, most women in the U.S. armed forces were nurses. The next-largest group of women were the Women's Army Corps (WAC): "Throughout the course of the war, about 700 WACs worked in Vietnam as stenographers, typists, clerks, air traffic controllers, cartographers, reporters, and photographers."⁹ When looking at the statistics of Vietnamese women, the numbers are less clear. It is believed that, in South Vietnam, around four thousand women joined the Women's Armed Forces Corps (a part of the ARVN), three thousand worked for the National Police, and more than one million Vietnamese women volunteered for the People's Self-Defense Forces.[10] North Vietnamese women fought in the PAVN and the NLF, as well as providing a massive amount of manual labor to maintain the Ho Chi Minh Trail. Conservative estimates suggest that up to 1.5 million women fought for North Vietnam.[11] But despite the official figures clearly showing that women *were* a huge part of the war, they remain a largely ignored group within American war comics.

In this chapter, I focus on the representation of women and girls, both American and Vietnamese. As women's roles in the U.S. military have changed and developed, so has their position within popular-culture representations. I interrogate the extent to which this comes through in comics of the war. One of the simplest explanations for the limited numbers of female protagonists in American comics of conflict is that women have long been considered only as bit players on the military stage; if women have not been able to take up these roles, then, naturally, they will not be depicted as frequently. However, this erases the massive labor undertaken by women in wartime, in both the public and private spheres, and limits what is considered "war" to the events of combat specifically.

In drawing the boundaries of what can be considered "war" (or "war content"), we can view the minimizing and silencing of women's experiences, voices, and labor as a part of preserving the perceived masculinity of the military. Though this is not something that is seen only during the Vietnam era, Susan Jeffords has argued that representations of the Vietnam War function as a space for traditional conceptions of masculinity that were, at the time, being challenged by the women's movement. For Jeffords, Vietnam is fertile cultural ground for what she calls "the remasculinization of America."[12] Comics follow the same trends seen in film, television, and literature, in their reinscription of male roles within warfare and, on a more abstract level, the "myth of the frontier" in which the redemption of American spirit or fortunes was "something to be achieved by playing through a scenario of separation, temporary regression to a more primitive or 'natural' state, and regeneration through violence."[13]

François Guillemot writes that the atrocities faced by women and girls were "all veiled in silence because the war was meant to be a people's war" and highlighting the voice of "the people" drowned out the myriad individual testimonies of women.[14] This gendered silence (and silencing) is heavily bound up in the cultures of silence that pervade the history of women and gender relations. For women in the United States, silence was built into the laws that governed the country from its colonization. Jane Brox writes that "in colonial America the presumption of silence was reinforced by women's subordinate place in society, and bolstered by centuries of English common law," wherein on marriage "the very being or legal existence of the woman is suspended."[15] Women's political and social voices were subsumed into the person of their husband or, if they were unmarried, remained with their fathers. More literally, "one set of laws . . . was aimed specifically at muting [women's] voices: Women could be harshly punished and humiliated simply for talking too much or too publicly or in a tone of voice that seemed grating or nagging."[16] American society (and indeed Western society) has developed with these laws at its root and as a foundational part of the roles of half the population. That this silence has crept into all aspects of life, both public and private, including the military, makes sense. And furthermore, that it underpins the representation of women in cultural documents is also logical.

Here I view women through three distinct lenses: the commodity, the combatant, and the caregiver. To what extent do female characters fill these three roles? Are they viewed through different lenses by different male characters? And where does silence enter the comics—how and why are women silenced here? Before turning to the three roles outlined above, I first must consider an enduring but often ignored aspect of the war that cuts across these three roles and permeates the gender politics of the war as a whole: the use of rape as a weapon against women and girls.

"Pretty SOP": Picturing Sexual Violence and War Rape

In her germinal study of rape, Susan Brownmiller writes, "War provides men with the perfect psychological backdrop to give vent to their contempt for women. The maleness of the military—the brute power of weaponry exclusive to their hands, the spiritual bonding of men at arms, the manly discipline of orders given, and orders obeyed, the simple logic of the hierarchical command—confirms for men what they long suspect—that women are peripheral to the world that counts."[17] For Brownmiller, war gives an opportunity for the baser desires of man's psyche to become reality. She suggests that the military is an intrinsically male institution, designed to accommodate and play into essentialist ideas of masculinity. It is also a situation wherein rapists are likely to remain unpunished. Although rape as a weapon is widely denounced as both a crime against humanity and an act of genocide, it is difficult to punish, given the scale of the act and the complexity of prosecution for these types of crimes. She goes on to say that "men who rape in war are ordinary Joes, made unordinary by entry into the most exclusive male-only club in the world."[18]

In a conflict where "ordinary Joes" made up a considerable proportion of the fighting forces, rape became commonplace.

Despite the prevalence of rape as a central aspect of many thousands of women's personal narratives of the war, it has remained largely ignored in American military documents and histories. At times, this ignoring seems more like erasure. For example, though many women and girls were raped during the Mỹ Lai massacre on March 16, 1968, this detail was downplayed in Seymour Hersh's influential reporting on the event. During the Winter Soldier Investigation in 1971, numerous soldiers spoke about witnessing horrific acts of sexual violence against Vietnamese women. In her study of this subject, Gina Weaver quotes one veteran who recalled "routine searches [during which] the women would have all their clothes taken off and the men would use their penises to probe them."[19] It was, as one veteran claimed, "Pretty SOP"–standard operating procedure; it is part of the basic furniture of combat.[20] Rape exists, and it is recognized but remains in the background of the war's larger narratives.

What about popular culture, and specifically comics? Where does rape feature in these narratives, and how does it play out? There are prominent rape scenes in many films and novels about the war. They follow the same basic narrative shape. A group of American men capture a young Vietnamese woman and rape and murder her. The story follows what was likely the typical event experienced by many thousands of women. But within popular culture, there has been some pushback. One review of Larry Heinemann's award-winning novel *Paco's Story* (1987) explicitly criticizes the rape scene: "The story itself is kind of an amalgam of clichés from the popular culture's rather deranged view of the war. In particular, there's one scene in which he participates in a gang rape that is purely obligatory. I'm hesitant to simply dismiss it as pandering, but one senses that it is there because Heinemann thinks the reader expects it to be."[21] This reviewer's suggestion that the reader expects a rape scene completely ignores the fact that we expect it *because* it is a common aspect of many veteran testimonies and their subsequent pop-culture representations. Rape in war, especially in the Vietnam War, is not a cliché and has nothing to do with a "deranged view"; it was and remains a wartime reality and one that popular-culture representations *do* engage with, though not always in the most appropriate, nuanced, or accurate ways. Though rape scenes occur frequently, they are portrayed as being in some way exceptional—the result of a particularly sadistic soldier or the culmination of a long-fought, sexualized battle. As Weaver writes, making the act the exception rather than the rule is akin to "erasing evidence of militarized masculinity's violent excesses, which had been highlighted by veteran literature and testimony," while also vilifying "Vietnamese women and [posing] American men as the true victims."[22]

In the rape-as-exceptional narrative, soldiers become traumatized heroes, rather than brutal victimizers, a reworking of characterization that speaks to the presumed facts that winners write the history and that, in turning these real-life experiences into marketable stories, audiences need to identify with the hero. What this does to the victims is a double silencing. Feminist studies and voices on rape have long argued that rape is a mechanism by which women are "kept in their place."[23] It is a crime, not of sex, but of power, which dehumanizes the victim and reinforces the power of the attacker. There is a tremendous amount of shame that is often experienced by rape victims, and "it is therefore not surprising that rape survivors often remain silent about their experiences."[24] Through the associated shame and silencing of rape victims, silence becomes emblematic of social powerlessness.[25] When rape occurs within wartime and is perpetrated against captured women by groups of male enemy forces, the act of rape takes on an additional level of power and violence. As Loren Kleinman writes, "Silence is the language of rape," and we can see this silence, inherent in the fabric and cultural reception of the crime, as the first level of silencing.[26] The second level comes within the representational form at hand. Were these rape victims American women attacked by Vietnamese (or other enemy) forces and saved by men, they would be given far more attention; the focus would still not be on them as victims, but on their male rescuers. However, they may be offered more space to speak than their Vietnamese sisters, who are given no space at all. None of the victims of rape in these comics utter a single word. They are not formed characters as much as plot devices that allow men to act and react.

There are three scenes in comics of the war that are emblematic for both their representation of violence against women and how it sits in relation to the wider conflict. In two of the three, the event is used as character development for the men. The women do not feature as anything more than a voiceless victim. In the third, the visual iconography of rape is used in a scene that does not, in fact, contain a rape. I contend that the rape imagery in this scene is used as a visual shortcut for the power and gender dynamics at play within the scene.

In *Vietnam Journal* 14, "Cordon and Search" (1990), Journal discovers that women from the village are being force-fed alcohol; the perpetrators pour "Johnnie Walker Red down [them] like soda pop."[27] Once drunk, the women are gang-raped in a truck by a succession of soldiers in full view of the camp before being taken away. Though not explicitly stated, the implication is that the women are murdered and their bodies are dumped unceremoniously. The attack on one woman is recounted to Journal by a soldier, Apple, who witnessed it and did nothing, claiming he was frozen in shock. At no point during the event does the woman speak, nor is her full body shown. She is merely a silent collection of female body parts. When asked why he did not speak up, Apple says, "I couldn't do that, they're my friends."[28] Once again, the male domination of the military space prevails over typical codes of morality and decency—to go against one's comrades is a greater crime than rape.

Later in the issue, a group of women suspected to be NLF are captured; they are held by ARVN soldiers. Apple follows them and finds that the women are being raped; he states, "Not again. I won't let it happen again."[29] Apple and Journal fight off the ARVN soldiers and stop the attack. Again, the women are barely shown and do not speak. All verbal interaction is between men. Apple is praised for his actions. The first sergeant tells him that "we may be involved in a war, but rape and torture are never justified. You made a stand against what you knew was wrong and to hell with the cost. I admire that."[30] The whole rape narrative is positioned as character development for Apple, with no concern given to the victims whatsoever. Apple, who was not prepared to break codes of brotherhood in the ranks to speak up against American rapists, speaks out only when the perpetrators are not his compatriots. In actuality, Americans were more likely to commit rape than their ARVN colleagues: "The presence of the wives and a general availability of sex (the brothel system has been a traditional part of Vietnamese society) gave ARVN soldiers less cause to rape."[31] Arguably, the hierarchy here is different. Rape in war exerts dominance over the enemy, to show enemy men that they have lost control over their women. The hierarchy differential has nothing to do with the availability of sex. Instead, this differential exposes rape as a weapon of war, and the ARVN are not at war with their own women. Though Apple's act is framed as an act of courage, it is not. It is further evidence of the erasure of women's experiences of conflict in general and war rape in particular. Furthermore, it is an example of the white racial frame at play in these comics.

Representations of rape are rarely about the women who are victims of the act; instead, they are about the men who perpetrate it and witness it. The second and third scenes for consideration are both taken from the Punisher's tour in Vietnam. While there is only an explicit rape event in one of the two, the overtones of sexual domination and violence against women is clear in both (see figures 6 and 7). In *The Punisher: Born* (2011), a young NLF sniper is caught by the platoon; one of the group, McDonald, begins to anally rape her. Figure 6 shows the panel of this act, and it is evident from the position of her feet and his bare buttocks that she is face down in the dirt. At no point does this woman speak. Captain Frank Castle shoots the woman in the head and states, "No rape. We're here to kill the enemy. That's all."[32] Later, McDonald is washing her blood off his face in a nearby lake when Castle drowns him. A naive young soldier, Stevie Goodwin, observes all of this from behind a tree. Castle explains to Goodwin that his shooting of the woman was an act of kindness—to save her life would only prolong her suffering. Goodwin narrates that he is afraid of Castle "because of the look he has in his eyes . . . and because what he did to that girl today was his idea of helping her out."[33] According to Robert Kodosky, "Castle demonstrates a twisted sense of mercy and morality in the field, prefiguring the odd moral code he adopts as the Punisher."[34]

For Brownmiller, rape can be seen as a logical course of action for a reassertion of power among male soldiers who are unable to seize control in a military arena. Through this lens, we can see the rape as McDonald (and, by extension, the rest of the patrol) regaining control of the landscape and reasserting their masculinity. War rape gives average men a way to be

6. Castle kills a woman in a "mercy killing" to remove her from the suffering of her rape at the hands of American soldiers. *The Punisher: Born*, Ennis, Robertson, and Palmer, 2011. © Marvel. Image presented under fair use legislation.

"something." The male body in this panel quite literally obscures the woman's body, leaving only her feet visible, thus placing focus on the men; the emphasis is on the traumatic response of the male witnesses. In purposely not positioning her within the image, the focus of the event is the traumatization of the men, leaving the complex issue of her trauma unspoken and unrepresented. The focus is on Castle's characterization in the situation, which has been contrived for him to do certain things that will show certain traits.

The final scene I turn to is in *Punisher: The Platoon*. Later in this chapter I will discuss the role of Ly, an NLF sniper who is seeking revenge for the murder of her family, but first I turn to her death. At the climax of the comic, having demonstrated tremendous mental and physical stamina, as well as courage, to reach this point, Ly is now in hand-to-hand combat with Castle. He is considerably larger than she is, yet the fight scene between them reveals their personal strengths up until the final image and death scene. As shown in figure 7, the death of Ly is visually similar to the rape of the NLF sniper in *Born*, as both women are shown only as feet and they are obscured by the men's bodies. However, there are three distinct differences in the representation of the two women's attacks that highlight the difference between Castle and McDonald. While McDonald rapes and dehumanizes his victim, Castle does not; he fights fair.

First, Ly is facing upward; she can make eye contact with Castle as she dies. There is a modicum of human connection in the ability to look someone in the eye, compared to the impersonal and distancing act of an attack from behind. Second, while McDonald is pressing down on top of the sniper (his bare buttocks indicating the act of penetration), there is no genital contact between Castle and Ly. There is a distinct space between them, as shown in figure 7. Finally, Castle kills Ly by slitting her throat, as evinced by the knife and slash of blood

7. Castle and Ly fight to the death, ending in a semisexual act of domination. *Punisher: The Platoon*, Ennis and Parlov, 2017. © Marvel. Image presented under fair use legislation.

visible to the left of his body in the image. It is not a penetrative stabbing, which would be more clearly suggestive of rape, but more akin to the clean slaughter of an animal. It is also an act of silencing, as a slash to the throat will invariably damage the vocal cords. She may not be sexually violated, but Ly is still silenced.

The reason that this distinction is crucial to the reading of these two panels is what they say about the position of the women. The sniper has said nothing, has been given no name, and is murdered face down by a gunshot wound. She is disposable, and her trauma is erased, instead becoming a catalyst for both Goodwin's and Castle's later actions and traumata. Ly, on the other hand, has been treated by her compatriots as their equal; her gender does not discredit her in any way. Castle treats her likewise as a worthy adversary and viable threat. Ly has been a disruptive force up until this point, as she stands in stark opposition to the fiercely masculine world of the U.S. military. Though her death is not an act of sexual violence, the overall visual presentation *does* suggest rape. It is only on looking closer that the distinction is made clear. However, this becomes moot. In death, with her voice silenced, Ly becomes another murdered woman as her agency and strength are erased.

"Everything's for Sale": Women as Commodity

The sex worker is the most common role given to Vietnamese women in pop-cultural representations of the war. The young woman I reference in the introduction to this chapter speaks to the visibility of the sex worker as a part of the American experience of the war. And while the truth of the matter is that there *were* large numbers of women who took up these roles, it is more nuanced than an initial glance may show. Estimates claim that five hundred thousand women worked as sex workers who sold sex.[35] Prostitution was officially illegal in South Vietnam; in 1967 the *New York Times* reported that more than three hundred women and fifty pimps were arrested in Nha Trang.[36] Unofficially, "prostitution was a lucrative form of finance for the government who allegedly took 30% of the proceeds from prostitution in the closed, off-limits prostitution zones which developed outside of the military brothels and bases."[37] Many women turned to sex work after being sexually assaulted or raped. Le Ly Hayslip recounts her own experience in her 1989 memoir: "Many of these girls . . . were rape victims like me who despaired of a proper marriage."[38] Stripping women of their agency and denying them full access to public life leads to sex work being the only option for any kind of employment (and protection).

As a term, "sex work" most commonly suggests a woman who engages in sex acts (including intercourse) for money. This is only one part of it, and sex work also encompasses those who do not engage in intercourse but are still using their bodies to entertain men in sexual or semisexual ways, a role taken up in vast numbers by bar girls. While not specifically selling intercourse, bar girls "worked in bars where their job was to charm American soldiers into buying them expensive drinks."[39] The bars sold Saigon tea, a fruity nonalcoholic drink. Soldiers would buy the drink for the bar girl, and she would receive half of the cost. If bar girls wanted to go home with the soldier, they were free to do so but at their own risk. Mai Lan Gustafsson writes that "Saigon was a paradise. The city offered what their villages could not: excitement, independence, novelty, and the exotic. They were not alone but were surrounded by more experienced workers who showed them the ropes and helped them find housing and work."[40]

The women (and girls—not all were over eighteen) who took up sex work of all kinds do not necessarily view their experiences in a negative light. It offered them a way out of rural life and presented them with opportunities that would have previously been unavailable. The stories of the war that come from this community give us a vastly different narrative from the "norm." They are stories of friendship, community, entrepreneurship, and survival in a male-dominated war zone.[41] The players in these stories are not *just* "prostitutes"; they have rich, individual experiences and stories. They are victims of the war and speak of their survival during this period with courage and tremendous strength.

These narratives are not a part of the U.S.-centric story of the war; these women and girls are given no space to speak. Instead, these women are framed as objects for the pleasure and consumption of (white, American) men; if their stories are told, they are framed as the stories of their American sexual partners or (usually) male pimps. Commodified women exist as part of the background in urban scenes, dressed in their typical uniform of short skirt and revealing top. When they do speak, however, they are the downfall of American men, either literally or morally. In *The 'Nam* 3, Ed Marks spends his three-day pass in Saigon. In a bar with two other soldiers, he meets a bar girl and buys her Saigon tea.[42] She takes him outside to "take a walk," and he is attacked by her pimp. Later that evening, Ed has a nightmare in which the sex worker features heavily.[43] Not only is she positioned as the (almost) cause of his death, but she is also central to the beginnings of his war trauma. This woman is a narrative device to show the naiveté of Ed and becomes a stand-in for all Vietnamese sex workers within *The 'Nam*: dangerous to American soldiers, devious, and unscrupulous.

The "No Mercy in Vietnam" arc ran in *Our Fighting Forces* from April 1966 to February 1967 and followed Captain Phil Hunter, as he tries to find his missing identical twin, Nick.[44] It is an unusual war comic in that it barely covers the war. Though there are elements of a war narrative throughout, it is not essential to the narrative that it occur in Vietnam or during this conflict. It is much more a story of the search efforts for Nick Hunter. The character of Lu Lin (also called "Kewpie Doll") is in many ways a commodified woman and one who occupies several parallel roles.[45] Lu Lin is a waitress in a Saigon bar (it is not implied that she is a bar girl); she is saved from a bombing in the café by Captain Hunter and vows to assist him in his search for his brother. They travel together through the Vietnamese jungle. At all times, she is dressed in a red *áo dài*, high heels, and *nón lá*; she carries her handbag over one shoulder, even during firefights. Lu Lin is the delicate, "exotic" love interest whose life is saved by the strong, masculine American. However, Hunter is unsure whether she is trustworthy or leading him into a trap. Her position oscillates throughout the arc, sometimes even between panels, as Hunter goes from kissing her to doubting her motives.

Lu Lin's key role—as clearly indicated by the nickname Hunter gives her—is to be the tempting love interest. In naming her after a doll, she is viewed as a toy, as something that is delicate and feminine. Although Lu Lin is present throughout the arc, she rarely speaks and only does so to offer comfort and support to Hunter. She follows him out of a sense of duty, since he saved her life, and she is devoid of agency herself. None of her actions are made to benefit herself or without consideration for Hunter's final goal of finding his brother. Though there is no exchange of money, Lu Lin is still commodified, as well as both a love interest and a potential downfall. Hunter refers to her on two occasions as a "cool almond cookie."[46] And following on from the discussion in chapter 1, she is represented with an alarmingly yellow skin tone.

Lu Lin is not a sex worker (at least, not explicitly). Many comics that include female characters in this role do not label them as such, especially if the series is covered by Comics Code Authority (CCA) guidelines, as I discuss in due course. Some do, however; Don Lomax's series *Vietnam Journal* features two interactions with sex workers. In the issue "Birds of Prey," Journal is approached by a sex worker who asks for blue jeans as payment for sex. She repeats the line, "We go boom-boom, you go PX, buy me jeans?"[47] She is not discerning, despite telling Journal, "Don't leave! I love you! You no love me?"[48] This woman, like the sex worker in *Full Metal Jacket* (and many others), is pathetic. She is desperate for a pair of jeans and is selling her body to receive them. To the soldiers, she is a figure of mild ridicule, and they mock her. Her desperation is funny to them and is positioned as funny within the comic. In the panel following her declaration of love to Journal, she is reciting her line to another soldier, while looking at him doe-eyed. But she is successful in the end. In the final panel of the comic, Journal asks a soldier how much a pair of jeans costs. He is prepared to solicit her services, and her line has worked. Though it is barely a transgression on his part, that the previously morally upright Journal would engage the services of a sex worker suggests a moral slippage that while not his downfall, does peel back some part of the veneer of respectability that covers him.

There are no comics that give proper voice to Vietnamese sex workers. At no point is their experience of the war discussed in a nuanced way; their motivations and viewpoint are not given space. There are many reasons for this. First, simply, the vast majority of these comics are created by white Americans living in the United States, with no knowledge of Vietnamese culture or people and no contact with Vietnamese sex workers. In other words, there was no access to these women's direct stories. Furthermore, these creators are mostly male, and they "typically demonstrated a weak understanding of women's distinctive voices and experiences."[49] Finally, many of these comics were published under the strict rules of the CCA, which banned "illicit sex relations," "seduction and rape," "sex perversion," and any kind of "profanity, obscenity, smut, [or] vulgarity."[50] Under these guidelines, any storyline presenting sex work required heavy self-censorship.

Only one comic has a sex worker "protagonist": *Hearts and Minds: A Vietnam Love Story* (1991). The term "protagonist" is not fully fitting for the character of Nhi, who is stuck between two men and whose actions lack any agency outside these relationships. When the story opens in 1965, Nhi and her husband Le live in an area of the Mekong Delta that is controlled by the NLF. After American soldiers find weapons, Le tries to run but is shot and presumed dead. The rest of the village, including Nhi and their child (a babe-in-arms), are evacuated. There is a time jump in which the reader is introduced to an American soldier, Lieutenant Jim Brett, and the two stories converge in the meeting room of a Hue brothel. Brett chooses Nhi as his "treat," and they spend the night together. He quickly falls in love and proposes marriage; she accepts. The story's climax comes during the Battle of Hue, when Le reappears as a member of the NLF and shoots Brett dead. Rather than being pleased that her husband is alive, Nhi is furious at him for what she perceives as abandonment and dies by gunshot; it is unclear whether she shoots herself or coerces him into shooting her.

Although the story follows Nhi, it is not Nhi's story. She remains under the control and "ownership" of men and masculine desire at all times; her actions are not governed by her own agency but by the patriarchal social, racial, and political structures that direct the war. On first meeting, Brett comments on Nhi's back, which is marked with scars. She coyly replies that "the Major has . . . special tastes."[51] There is no sense of disgust to her words, and she makes an offhand comment about the other sex workers who have been similarly beaten. Immediately after this is spoken, Nhi is pictured lying naked, flat on her back, looking expectantly at Brett. At no point during this exchange does Nhi betray any hint that she is not a willing participant in it. It would be incorrect to say that women who engage in sex work are all unwilling, but Nhi's demeanor is one of total submission. She portrays the stereotypical Asian woman as seen through American eyes—beautiful and submissive, simultaneously pure and a whore. To complicate her physical characterization, Nhi is half-French; this makes her "exotic" to her clients. However, she is drawn with a Caucasian facial structure and blue eyes. Her ethnicity is not explained at all. Although detailed figures are not known, it is assumed that the numbers of children born of Vietnamese mothers and French fathers were not insignificant; the Vietnamese term for these children is *con lai* ("mixed race"). During the French occupation, these children were not always treated kindly, a sign of fraternization with the enemy. Rather than drawing on this history, Nhi's heritage simultaneously codes her as more exotic to Vietnamese clients and more acceptable to Americans.

Nhi is mostly pictured either naked or wearing formfitting, translucent clothing. This is to be expected, given that she is a sex worker, but she alone is presented in this way. Brett remains fully clothed or is covered by a sheet. On the large number of female nudes in Western art, compared to the relative dearth of male nudes, John Berger writes that "a man's presence is dependent upon the promise of power which he embodies."[52] Brett's uniform is a visual representation of the power he embodies—the power of the American armed forces. Nhi's power is solely contained within her physicality: "To be born a woman has been to be born, within an allotted and confined space, into the keeping of men."[53] Nhi's nudity is not only part of her work uniform, but it is the confined space in which she is able to exist as a woman. Her extremely narrow plane of existence is literally worn on her skin; it is her only way to exert power in any tangible way. However, this appears moot when she, post coitus, discusses her "purchase" from the brothel by Brett. He states, "I bought you! You're mine now!" Though she replies, "Yes Master!" in a jocular tone, the power dynamics between a white American man and a Vietnamese sex worker are undeniably *not* in her favor.[54] The slave does not, by definition, hold power.

Nhi, Le, and Brett all die when the three collide during the Battle of Hue. Brett abandons his men in the middle of the battle to search for Nhi. Despite it being Brett's choice, Nhi can be positioned as a corrupting influence, as she has caused a rupture in the central relationship within the military—between brothers-in-arms. Le bursts into the room as Nhi and Brett embrace and shoots Brett dead. Nhi refuses to accept her husband and asserts that he is the one who should be dead, that he abandoned her and their child, and that he is the reason for her turning to sex work. Rather than being stripped of her agency by others, Nhi is removing it for herself by acknowledging her position within the patriarchal war machine. She is divesting herself of her own agency and makes a move to regain it by turning a gun on Le. His response ("No! Don't make me!") and the ambiguous image leaves it unsaid whether Nhi's death was an act of suicide or homicide.[55] She dies draped in a suggestive position on top of the fully clad Brett, with one breast exposed. In death, as in life, she is a sexualized nude body. Returning to Nguyen's words from the introduction to this chapter, Nhi embodies the woman who "willingly [dies] for the love of white men."[56]

Flowers on the Frontlines: Women as Combatants

If one side of the representational coin with respect to Vietnamese women's roles is sex workers, the other side is combatants.[57] Women in both North and South Vietnam worked in a wide range of roles within the military, unlike American women, who were confined to a small number of functions, mostly nursing or desk roles.[58] In the final section of this chapter, I examine nurses; American women in other military roles do not exist within comics of the Vietnam war. But first, I turn to women who take on an active combat role—in terms of appearances in comics, this refers to North Vietnamese women, both PAVN and NLF.

The North Vietnamese government under Ho Chi Minh was, in many ways, progressive, especially in relation to women's rights and gender equality. The role of women in society was championed as an important part of industrial and economic growth; new laws banned forced marriage and child marriage, while also instigating harsh punishment for domestic abuse.[59] Positioning women as active players in social development meant that it was seen as natural for women also to take on roles within the military; they were often employed laying booby traps or working in the extensive tunnel network or in espionage (women were able to move much more freely than men in many areas of the country with heavy U.S. presence).[60] There are few accurate data available, but some estimates suggest that at least 1.5 million women served in the North Vietnamese military.[61] William Turley writes, "One of the great accomplishments claimed by the [Communist Party of Vietnam] is the emancipation of women from oppressive feudal social structures and attitudes and the establishment of equality between the sexes. The publicity given to women's achievements in the Democratic Republic of Vietnam (DRV), the importance of posts held by women in the government and the presence of women among communist delegations abroad lend support to this claim."[62] He goes on to add that "the percentage of women in village militia was estimated to have grown from 10% to 22% in 1965 alone and to have reached 30% by the end of 1966 with some village units composed of over 50% women."[63] But despite the necessary work of women and their acceptance in the military, there was still rampant sexism and a gendered division of labor in camps, as well as regulations against women working with American and ARVN soldiers. One of the most visible examples of this sexism is found in propaganda that highlighted femininity and called these soldiers the "flowers on the frontline."[64]

Among the most iconic and influential figures in Vietnamese history are the Trưng sisters. Trưng Trắc and Trưng Nhị are heralded as heroes in Vietnam, often depicted riding an elephant. In the year 40 CE, they led the Vietnamese military to victory against the Chinese and ruled for three years, before being defeated and beheaded by Chinese general Ma Yuan. Their gender not only places them within the pantheon of female warriors, many of whom are central figures within national and cultural mythologies, but was likely the reason for their rebellion's eventual failure. According to Keith Weller Taylor, Trưng Trắc's soldiers, "seeing that she was a woman, feared she could not stand up to the enemy and consequently dispersed."[65] Despite the failure of the rebellion, the sisters remain central to Vietnamese histories of women and resistance.

With so many women working within the military, we would expect to see more of them in combat roles in comics of the conflict, but this is distinctly not the case. Comics of the 1950s and 1960s contain few women in combat. Featured women are background characters, usually mothers with babies in arms, running from a bomb strike on their village. The lack of women in these comics makes sense when we consider that no American women would have held combat roles at that time, which means it is highly likely that comics writers would not know that Vietnamese women did not face the same restrictions—a projection of U.S. patriarchy and gender formation instead of a representation of a real place. Alternatively, they may have been aware of the roles of Vietnamese women but felt that including Vietnamese women soldiers would not be understood by American readers and would have been contrary to American social mores and gender roles. The removal of women in combat can be seen as an extension of the silencing of Vietnamese men, as discussed in chapter 1.

In comics published since 1975, women and girls do take on combat roles. Jason Aaron and Cameron Stewart's *The Other Side* includes a woman as a guide for the PAVN soldiers; she appears briefly as they traverse a particularly dangerous area of the jungle at night, by candlelight. Her speech is intense: "This is the road to heartache and eternal pain. This is the road to ruin, desecration, and the perversion of all that is holy. This is the road to war."⁵⁶ Her words are reminiscent of the words above the gates of hell in Dante's *Commedia*: "I am the way to the City of Weeping. I am the way to eternal pain. I am the way among the lost."⁶⁷ Her voice and her words are bold and powerful. She is scarred by her experiences within the war, but it has made her tough. For the guide, war is hell, and hell is upon them.

The guide in *The Other Side* has no name and makes only a brief appearance, albeit a memorable one. In *Punisher: The Platoon* the character of Ly is not only granted a name, but she is positioned as the antagonist opposite Frank Castle and given both voice and agency. The comic, published as a miniseries across six issues, follows Castle as a young man in his first tour in Vietnam. The Vietnam story is framed by two present-day narratives: interviews with Castle's former platoon, who talk about Castle, and a North Vietnamese general, who talks about Ly. During his tour, Castle begins to develop the peculiar morality that epitomizes the Punisher. But to Ly Quang, a young woman in the NLF, he is the symbol of everything that has already destroyed and continues to ruin Vietnam.⁶⁸

When Ly is first introduced, she is sitting on a bed while being treated by a medic, after having been injured in a firefight. She is dressed in black *áo bà ba* and has wildly unkempt hair. Though *áo bà ba* is worn by both genders, the garments worn by women tend to be of brighter colors and more delicate fabrics than Ly's. Her masculine choice of dress and her messy hair is juxtaposed to her soft, delicate features and large brown eyes. Visually, she is the coming together of masculinity and femininity. Colonel Giap addresses her as "sister," and it becomes clear that she is a renegade and that the colonel is treating her carefully to afford respect for her obvious skill and courage but also to impart his superior wisdom gently. Theirs is a mentor-student relationship, and Ly's narrative is a coming-of-age story.

In a later scene, on the eve of her final fight with Castle, Ly speaks with Colonel Giap one final time. She explains her personal history and the reasons behind her desperate all-consuming need for revenge against the Americans. Her father bound and gagged her, hiding her in a cellar, to save her from a search-and-destroy team. Instead of giving her up, her family were viciously murdered and mutilated, and Ly vowed revenge. Her motives are neither individualist nor nationalist—they are familial. It is not a concept that can be fully understood by the Americans, whose families are eight thousand miles away.[69] It would be easy—and not inaccurate—to view Ly as an avenging-angel character type. It would be similarly easy to suggest that she is apolitical but drawn into the war by her family's death: an accidental guerrilla who would rather be left alone but cannot ignore the atrocities within her own family. Both positions erase any political or ideological motivations. This is not an uncommon erasure of Vietnamese political agency; the belief that the Vietnamese (both North and South) were apolitical, apathetic, and lacked political guts remained a common position in U.S. popular culture, despite the obvious evidence to the contrary. As early as 1972, Jeffrey Race suggested that the Vietnamese were an intensely political and politicized nation and that, by 1965 and the arrival of U.S. military intervention, the NLF had already won the battle of hearts and minds.[70]

The conversation with Colonel Giap covers four pages. Each page is structured with bandeau panels of equal height. Ly speaks without interruption. Her words are placed in speech balloons over images of her speaking, and only one panel includes a flashback image of the bound and gagged Ly. Despite their difference in rank and gender, Giap allows Ly to speak freely. She does so with candor and honesty. At no point is she obscured by the male character. They are placed side by side as equals, fully faced, and clear. In this single scene alone, Ly is granted more agency over her own narrative than any other woman in Vietnam comics. In one panel, Giap speaks, and his words are in a bubble next to the image of Ly's face. We as readers are placed with her as if we were seeing from her position. We are invited to empathize with her. Ly's story is entirely her own, told in words that are either hers or couch her in immense respect, but the narrative framing asks us to place ourselves with her as much as with Castle. This is not a story of two clear-cut sides as much as a story of constantly shifting perspectives and moralities.

Regardless of their specific role, their motives, or their sacrifice, women combatants do not receive anywhere near the amount of attention within comics as would match the size of their involvement in the war. Ly is the only female combatant in these comics who receives equal narrative focus to her male counterparts. Though the statistics clearly show that women were integral to both military roles and infrastructure maintenance in North Vietnam and military support in South Vietnam, as I have already discussed in the introduction to this chapter, their labor is erased, and their voices are silenced in the U.S.-centric narrative. We may say that the roles in which women were employed are, by their nature, less visible, and so their invisibility in the comics is not unusual. But the total erasure of *all* roles (save for a few select exceptions that are in direct relation to U.S. servicemen) shows that the comics are tightly focused on Americans and the war as an American war.

Karen Turner-Gottschang and Thanh Hao Phan write, "Brave as they were to try to free the nation from oppressive native rulers and outside invaders, Vietnam's fighting women never enjoyed for long the fruits of their struggle or challenged seriously the dominant patriarchal culture."[71] Though this quotation refers to the patriarchal culture of the Vietnamese military, it can also be read in the light of comics' erasure and silencing of fighting women.

Angels with Smiling Faces: Women as Caregivers

The final role I examine in this trifecta of women's identities is the caregiver—those roles explicitly involved in the welfare of others, be it medical or domestic. Traditional gender roles place the heaviest caregiving burden on women, both in the workplace (in 1970, men made up only 2.7 percent of American nurses) and at home (in the early 1970s, American women spent an average of thirty-eight hours a week on domestic labor).[72] These same gender politics underpin the representation of American women within comics of the war. They are portrayed as angelic, regardless of their role; they are beautiful, delicate, and selfless. For the most part, these female characters occupy the role of nurse. In truth, most American women who served did so as nurses. Detailed figures are not available, but around 11,000 U.S. women were stationed in Vietnam, with a further 230,000 stationed in the United States.[73] The role was incredibly debilitating, between the harsh climate, lack of air-conditioning and (often) proper supplies, and grueling shifts. They were also expected to project a specific type of wholesome American femininity: "She might have been a nurse, but she was still needed for her touch, smile, and reassuring beauty."[74] Stur writes, "Military women such as nurses and Women's Army Corps personnel sometimes became stand-ins for the wives, girlfriends, mothers, and sisters of servicemen. It was the way in which troops made sense of American women being in places that were exclusively male, according to the popular culture they had grown up with, modern equivalents of the 'Indian country' where John Wayne and other cowboys protected their women and homesteads from savages."[75] In this popular-culture world, women are soft and fragile, in need of the macho protection of men, and lack their own agency. There is little acknowledgment of the massive amount of physically and mentally exhausting labor that was required of women in war zones, as either civilians or military personnel. Nurses would be expected to shoulder the combined burden of treating horrific injuries and counseling traumatized soldiers, while also presenting a pretty, smiling face. Rather than take on the complexities of their roles as nurses, many comics present nurses as silent and pretty, doing their jobs in the background without voice. There are few examples of nurse characters who have a speaking role, but at all times they remain within the tight boundaries of girl-next-door sweet femininity that is prescribed for them by the overarching gender-political structures of both the military and American social mores.

In 1962 and 1963 the long-running Charlton romance series *My Secret Life* was briefly retitled to *Sue and Sally Smith: Flying Nurses*. The twin nurses had featured in a special story arc in *My Secret Life* 47 before the retitling, which ran for seven issues.[76] The twins Sue and Sally, one blonde and one brunette, are nurses at the Morse Memorial Center, somewhere in the American Midwest, and volunteers for the Emergency Corps Rescue Team. Across seven issues, they participate in all manner of daring adventures, including rescuing (in midair) a man whose parachute did not open and skiing down an Alaskan mountain with a patient on a stretcher. Their compassion as nurses is matched only with their tremendous athleticism and poise under pressure. In a similar vein to the male special forces characters also popular in the early 1960s, Sue and Sally Smith are superheroic—their abilities go beyond what is typical, expected, or normal.

In *Sue and Sally Smith: Flying Nurses* 48, the story arc "Dangerous Assignment" follows Sue's trip to Vietnam to assist an injured doctor working in a hospital for orphaned children. Dressed in an impeccable blue uniform, with perfectly coiffed blonde curls and manicured nails, she cooks and cleans for the hospital, taking on a motherly role, with a soft and loving bedside manner. Though beautiful, she is sexless and faces none of the sexual harassment that testimonies state was a common issue for nurses. Sue fills many roles: mother to orphaned children, maid for the injured Dr. Tillman, nurse to the injured NLF soldier, and also innocent and fragile woman to be protected by her male colleagues, both American and ARVN. Though she is a skilled nurse, what is most highly valued is her representation of ideal American femininity. In many ways, she could be described as hyperfeminine. She stands in perfect contrast to the ideal American (hyper)masculinity of her Green Beret and MACV counterparts.

The cover image shows Sue Smith bandaging the leg of an injured man. Though it is not obvious by the image, this man is an NLF soldier. As I discuss in chapter 1, the visual presentation of Vietnamese characters is often unusual, and they are vaguely Other in their appearance and skin tone. This man has a thin, Fu Manchu–style mustache, highlighting the caricatured Asian appearance that was so typical of the time. The bandage that Sue is wrapping is lightly soaked in a blue substance, with no sign of any blood or damage to the man's leg whatsoever. There is no blood on Sue or the ground, though the man appears to be sweating slightly. But we must note that *Sue and Sally Smith* is not a war title; it is a romance title. The target audience is markedly different, being young women and girls. The storylines are therefore much gentler and more sanitized than in war comics. The other stories within the comic are typical romance narratives; it is only the cover story that has any war content at all. For the romance readership, a sudden burst of blood and guts would have been surprising, to say the least. Stories of nurses, in which they are the protagonists and the agents of the narrative, are directed at young women. Though their adventures may take place within war zones, Sue and Sally Smith exist at arm's length from the conflict and the world of men.

Despite the vast number of women who served as nurses in Vietnam—and their obvious importance to the war machine—*Sue and Sally Smith: Flying Nurses* is one of a small number of comics that show nurses as anything more than background characters. It is the only one published during the war period of which I am aware. In later comics, including *The 'Nam* and *Vietnam Journal*, nurses appear in hospital scenes, but they are bit players rather than protagonists. In *The 'Nam* 13 ("The Bombs Bursting"), cute freckle-faced Jane is the confidante of softhearted soldier Andy. Jane appears only twice—both times when Andy is visiting his injured comrades in the hospital. Her only role is to offer a comforting shoulder to Andy and to give short medical updates on the status of the soldiers' health. Though she speaks fewer than ten sentences, Jane is the only nurse who is given a voice in the entirety of the eighty-four-issue run. Similarly, in *Vietnam Journal* 7 ("Dustoff"), nurse Connie is a sounding board for Journal's concerns and, at the end of the issue, for a poem written about the war experience by an injured soldier, Pete.[77] Though Connie is not as "cute" as Jane (Connie wears fatigues, whereas Jane wears a traditional nursing uniform), she is still devoid of agency and voice in the same way. They are both mere decorations, serving and listening to men.

3
Broken Kites

Trauma and the Return

> Wars are not paid for in wartime. The bill comes later.
> —BENJAMIN FRANKLIN (ATTRIB.)

Billy Pilgrim, the "hero" of Kurt Vonnegut's 1969 novel *Slaughterhouse-Five*, is so traumatized by his experiences during World War II that he loses all grip on time. His fragile mental state is captured in time travel that permeates the novel but also in a singular image: a kite. In a POW camp, after watching a surreal performance of *Cinderella*, Billy accidentally sets fire to his coat. His rescuer, a British soldier, quips, "What have they done to you, lad? This isn't a man. It's a broken kite."[1] This image of brokenness is an effective analogy for a man suffering from the effects of conflict trauma. A kite, once broken and mended, may fly but will never be the same. It is forever changed by the experience.

In the aftermath of conflict, bodies and minds are left broken, and though they may appear fixed, the fault lines remain. However, even among the destruction and disconnection of war, we still find ways to connect, and the overwhelmingly human drive for connection endures. For Aristotle, "it is evident that the state is a creation of nature and that man by nature is a political animal."[2] The word "political" stems from the Greek word πόλις ("polis"), referring to a city-state. Aristotle saw humans not as political in the modern English sense of the word but as social animals. Our selves are defined by our relationship to a wider society; we exist *only* in connection to one another. And at their heart, war stories are about connection and disconnection. They are about the way that individuals act in extraordinary circumstances, the strategies and methods for survival that become a part of existing, and how that new existence affects our most basic impulses as humans—to be social and to exist in community. For Tim O'Brien, true war stories are "about love and memory."[3]

Christian Appy writes that, in the decade following the war, "if veterans were featured at all in movies or the press it was often as drug-addled and violent. [The stereotype of the] 'crazy vet' was infuriating to veterans."[4] Characters such as Rambo exemplified a range of negative stereotypes: "vet as psycho, vet as killer, vet as outcast, vet as victim," while representing a muscle-bound and intensely physical macho masculinity.[5] Appy notes that "nothing in these films did justice to the complexity of the war or those who fought it."[6] I would modify his statement slightly. While within his research corpus this is true, there *are* films from this period that engage with the complexity of the war, but they are not common. Moreover, they contain very little discussion of the "after." The figure of the soldier in theater is not ignored in popular culture, but the returned veteran largely is. And when they are present, the depictions follow a narrow model that is both instantly recognizable and mostly inaccurate. Here the silencing of the veteran begins as they are excluded from their *own* stories, as are the other groups I consider in this book. The lack of desire to make an accurate representation of trauma in these films—or to bring veterans with PTSD into the development process as advisors—demonstrates the lack of interest in accuracy and verisimilitude that sits at the core of these texts. Violent, deranged characters "sell better" and make for more dramatic and intense storytelling. The reality of trauma and PTSD is a slow and painful process of psychological growth and processing; it is not cinematic.

Though it is becoming less common with time, American popular culture is peppered with characters who are defined by their service in Vietnam and who are depicted in line with the aforementioned inaccurate model. They are typically men who would have been in their late teens or early twenties during the war; their service is visually defined by grizzled appearance, often wearing a bandana; their behavior is disturbed, hypervigilant, with occasional shots of their faces with a thousand-yard stare, over a faded background of helicopters and jungle landscapes. This visual shorthand is "'Nam," a metonym for the experience of warfare, injury, and trauma. These characters are overwhelmingly white cis men; they are violent, often dealing with substance abuse, and unable to function within "normal" society.[7] We see this in the characters of Travis Bickle in *Taxi Driver* (1976); Dan Taylor in *Forrest Gump* (1994); Walter in *The Big Lebowski* (1999); and, more recently, Mike Ehrmantraut in *Breaking Bad* (2008–13) and Jim Hopper in *Stranger Things* (2016–).[8] As the war recedes further into living memory, characters who are veterans—and whose personality and behavior are defined by their service—are even less common in media that are not directly focused on the war's aftermath.

But what of comics? Where do returning veterans appear in comics narratives of the war—is their role similar to that of their televisual siblings? How does the type of comic affect the representation? This chapter addresses these questions, while also considering the broader representation of trauma at play in comics about Vietnam. I begin with a much wider picture and a brief overview of the relationship between Vietnam and trauma, with a focus on the importance of this very conflict in the history of trauma as a medical diagnosis and military phenomenon and on how this specific history is made visible in comics about the war. I consider three primary case studies, using three distinct comics that focus on returning service members and their experience of both conflict and trauma. I focus first on the classic depiction of the returning veteran in the grips of severe psychotic trauma, in *Hellblazer* 5 (1988). Then I move on to consider how trauma can be a tool for bonding and connection between individuals with similar experiences, in *Enemy Ace: War Idyll* (1990). Finally, I turn to trauma as a national, collective response to the horrors of conflict, in *The Legion of Charlies* (1971).

Vietnam and Trauma

The Vietnam War is an important benchmark in the history and development of trauma as both a medical diagnosis and as a cultural phenomenon. This is not to say that trauma was an unknown experience prior to the mid-twentieth century. On the contrary, it is as old as violence, and we can see it represented in cultural artifacts that date back thousands of years. In *Henry IV, Part I*, Lady Percy recounts her husband's night terrors and evident combat trauma, in stark contrast to his battlefield nickname of "Hotspur."[9] Despite the long history of trauma as a human experience, there was remarkably little research into it prior to the works of Sigmund Freud, Josef Breuer, and Pierre Janet in the late nineteenth century, most notably Freud and Breuer's *The Aetiology of Hysteria* (1895). When research into trauma did begin, it focused on the pseudomedical concept of hysteria and took several decades to shake off the stigma of cowardice that unfortunately followed combat-related diagnoses of what was then labeled "shell shock."

During the First World War, 306 British men were executed for "cowardice," though it is now thought that they were suffering from what would later be recognized as PTSD.[10] After the war, Lord Gort gave testimony that labeled "shell shock" as a sign of bad character and weakness, not found in "good units."[11] "Proper" men do not develop trauma, because it is a sign of weakness and femininity; we see this connection in Freud and Breuer's early research, when trauma was linked to the uterus.[12] Though in clinical terms any link between trauma and cowardice is discredited, there remains an ever-present haunting of this past connection in popular representations of trauma. With the shift away from discourses of shame and cowardice, research focus has centered on combat, and that is where it settled.

In my 2017 study of war comics, I wrote at length about the representation of trauma and PTSD.[13] The inclusion of PTSD in the 1980 edition of the *Diagnostic and Statistical Manual of Mental Disorders* (DSM) ratified the condition and led to a considerable body of further research, most of which took returning U.S. veterans as their research subjects.[14] Thus, the vast majority of research into trauma and PTSD was conducted on a narrow, homogeneous group: white male soldiers who had returned from Vietnam. If this phenomenon was by no means a new one when the war ended in 1975, why, then, do I claim that Vietnam is a benchmark for representations of conflict? Speaking of Vietnam as a sociohistorical chronotope, it is the advent of a new phase in trauma-studies research; it signifies an important move forward in the classification and treatment of those who have experienced life-altering events, while also foreshadowing a more positive approach to the treatment of mental illness in general. Naming the phenomenon of conflict "trauma" and giving it a place within clinical and research communities gives us a new lens through which to frame representations of conflict, but it also has two key limitations that need to be recognized.

The first is the efficacy of the research scope. Much of the trauma theory that was developed from case studies of Vietnam veterans centered on a white, working-class, male experience. As I have discussed at length elsewhere, this narrow focus negates the experiences of members of minority groups and suggests that trauma arising from conflict can be conflated with all other traumatic experiences, including both acute and chronic personal violence, political terrorism, and natural disasters.[15] Though my textual focus here sits well within the temporal research parameters, the characters I am concerned with in earlier chapters do not. As I show throughout this study, there are more voices within the experiences of the war than just the few who are given space in trauma studies. Furthermore, Vietnam is generally considered to be the first conflict in which the U.S. military was fully racially integrated, although official integration had occurred in July 1948.[16] The research performed does not take into account the experiences of soldiers of color. It also does not cover the experiences of women who worked as nurses and in other noncombat roles and who were victims of sexual violence, as I discuss in chapter 2. I do not dismiss this body of research, despite its limitations. However, it is necessary to see how the research, as it was conducted at the time, affects the lay understanding of trauma and PTSD that we find in comics.

The second limitation sits with classic trauma studies, which consider trauma to be unspeakable, unrepresentable, and inherently unknowable. Beginning with Freud's work in the late nineteenth and early twentieth centuries, most notably *The Aetiology of Hysteria* (1896, written with Josef Breuer), *Beyond the Pleasure Principle* (1920), and *Moses and Monotheism* (1939), the classic model sees trauma as a Gordian knot that sits at the center of an individual's consciousness, refusing to be assimilated into "our understanding of a normal human experience—thus permanently keeping the traumatic experience apart from consciousness."[17] Anne Whitehead is succinct in her description of this unspeakability when she writes, "Trauma ... overwhelms the individual and resists language or representation."[18] This model does not allow for the personal nuances of trauma. Instead, contemporary, pluralistic trauma theory "challenges the traditional concept of trauma as unspeakable by starting from a standpoint that concedes trauma's variability in literature and society"; this model seeks to emphasize "that trauma occurs to actual people, in specific bodies, located within particular time periods and places."[19] The end point for this model is not perfect, positive healing but stability and a neutral place of balance and symptom management.

Comics representations of the soldiers' returns are overwhelmingly negative. These stories culminate in negative climaxes that are characterized by familial breakdown, extreme mental health crisis, and death. The classic understanding of trauma as unspeakable is among the most commonly shown tropes, which fits with the research that directly resulted from the war itself. Characters are unable to voice their traumatic experiences, which is the crux of their failure to reintegrate and to reach a position of stability. This *is* an effect of trauma, but it is only one among many. Far more common is the desperate need to speak about the experience but finding that there is no outlet for this. The individual is silenced by their surroundings, not by the trauma itself. The focus on this particular effect suggests universality. This is not the case, and the emphasis on it locates the returning veteran as a person who is broken beyond any repair or recovery. When this becomes the most seen version of the traumatized vet in popular culture, it is absorbed as being the way trauma looks in an individual. Those who do not display this specific set of symptoms are overlooked, belittled, or accused of lying about their time in combat. Survivors of noncombat traumata (such as natural disasters, sexual violence, and violent crime) are equally as likely as combat veterans to develop PTSD, yet it is often seen as a combat-only diagnosis.

Where do we see traumatized veterans in comics of the Vietnam War? In comics published during the war, they are absent. The reasons for this encompass both the nature of the comics themselves and the position of trauma within contemporaneous understanding of the effects of combat. Though there was medical treatment available for those suffering the effects of combat stress, the mechanics of trauma itself were little known; patients were often treated with sedatives and barbiturates. Treatment of trauma as a primarily psychological condition explicitly caused by exposure to combat was not typical until 1980, and so to view an individual's response as something medical (thus diagnosable and treatable) would be rare. The specific focus of these comics shifts as the nature of U.S. intervention shifts, but the overall emphasis remains the same—soldiers in theater, fighting in jungle spaces or enjoying R&R (rest and recuperation) in city spaces. To the best of my knowledge, there is only one comic published during the war that deals with returning veterans: *The Legion of Charlies* (1971), which I discuss later in this chapter.

Turning to comics about the war that were published in the 1980s, in both *The 'Nam* and *Vietnam Journal* only two instances of trauma are shown, which, given that both series are set primarily in-country, makes sense if we think of the afterwardsness of trauma.[20] In *The 'Nam* trauma is encapsulated in the character of Frank Verzyl. Verzyl, a former soldier and "tunnel rat" (someone who goes into the NLF tunnels to help destroy the network from within), is attacked by rats, and it triggers a serious psychotic break in him, leading to him killing his commanding officer. He is returned to the United

States and held in a psychiatric hospital; the final panel of his story shows a close-up of his face with wide and staring eyes, as he is restrained in a straitjacket. His eyes suggest that he is viewing something terrifying and life-threatening; the reader is seeing his reaction to what he is seeing. Though the psychotic break with reality and the traumatic symptoms begin in theater, Verzyl's portrayal of trauma at this point in the narrative is accurate. PTSD takes root *after* the event is complete. He is, to all intents and purposes, safe. The terror he is experiencing is that which his mind is playing on a loop, without active comprehension, suggesting a severe psychotic detachment, which is not a common symptom but does occur, coupled with catatonia. He is trapped in that moment, and the terror in his eyes is the terror of a traumatized man, the only one in eighty-four issues of the series.

Vietnam Journal takes a different approach to representing trauma in that the traumatic experience and response are faced by the protagonist, rather than a side character, and he is still in theater when his symptoms begin. During a firefight in a rice paddy, where one soldier loses a limb and another dies, Journal is severely injured and almost disemboweled.[21] While recuperating in a Saigon hospital, he hallucinates and sees bloodied bodies pressing against the windows. The vision passes quickly and is not mentioned again; it is the only symptom of trauma that he appears to suffer.[22] He recovers quickly, and at no point in the remaining eight issues of the series is trauma mentioned again. The inclusion of the scene is unusual, given that the singular traumatic symptom appears and disappears within a page. Journal returns to the United States soon after and there faces a crisis of conscience when he is trying to decide whether or not to return to Vietnam. The traumatic hallucination is a plot device only to give a reason to remove him temporarily from theater. His traumatic response is not a necessary part of his experience in Vietnam, nor is it a foundational event that affects his life going forward. It is simply a plot device.

Unlike in *The 'Nam*, which sought to represent the war accurately (albeit for only a tiny percentage of those involved) and where the traumatized individual is shown to be deeply affected, *Journal* is only momentarily upset. Given that these are the only two long-running series about the Vietnam War, their lack of engagement with the aftermath of the conflict is notable; just as these series do not give space to women or Vietnamese characters, they also exclude the returners. They are not an important part of the Vietnam War narrative in these comics. Interest in the war dies as the returning planes are taking off. The failure of the U.S. military to adequately treat and protect their service members after their tours were done is perhaps one of the greatest failures of the war.[23]

Even though these characters are few and far between, their existence raises some complex and potentially uncomfortable questions for readers, in relation not only to the texts but also to their own understanding of the narrative of Vietnam and our response to it. Why is this representation of the traumatized veteran the one that persists, even when there is myriad evidence to show that it is not an accurate portrayal and, moreover, that many veterans themselves are displeased by it? And why do we as viewers have little interest in seeing the characters engaging with and working through their traumata? The simplest answer here is that such storylines are just not that interesting . . . at least, not as sustained narratives. But more importantly, Vietnam is not a war with clearly defined players; it is not a war with "good guys" and "bad guys." It is far more comfortable for audiences to ignore parts of the war experience that show their compatriots, their government, and potentially their loved ones in a negative light.

Consider this: a character who has had awful experiences in

BROKEN KITES 111

theater comes home with profound mental health concerns, struggles with substance abuse, and cannot hold down a job. This character is easy to visualize, but once we peel away the top layer, we are compelled to ask why this person is like this. What did they experience? Perhaps they witnessed one of their brothers-in-arms commit murder and rape. This complicates the binary of victim and perpetrator to include witnesses and then emphasizes the witness's lack of action in preventing the acts. Perhaps they themselves were involved in the deaths of civilians. The trauma of something that you are responsible for, at least in some small part, is an extraordinarily complex trauma to work through. This is not to say that *all* American service members engaged in this kind of action against civilians; yet it was widespread enough that a substantial number were. There is intense complexity in the ways these men experienced and will continue to experience their traumata, complicated by feelings of guilt and shame, but this is missing from popular-culture renderings of events during and after the war.

In the introduction to this book, I argued that the removal of accurate representation demonstrates the erasure of American culpability in atrocity and a lack of awareness of the need to confront the full weight of U.S. involvement in Vietnam. In a forthcoming article on comics remediations of the Mỹ Lai massacre, I describe the overarching narrative of the massacre within comics, which places blame on one individual—Lieutenant William Calley.[24] Though Calley was both the superior of the men involved and a participant in the massacre, the orders came from officers above him. However, these men escaped scrutiny, and Calley was made to take all blame. The extreme simplification of the narrative was tremendously useful to the U.S. Army, who were (briefly) absolved of blame, in labeling Calley as the solo "bad egg."

What does this simplification of the representation of veterans' trauma and experience mean for the narrative of the war? It means that the narrative being put forward in American cultural artifacts—be they visual, written, or aural—are building on an understanding of trauma that not only is medically incorrect but also has the potential to be harmful to those who are experiencing PTSD or PTS. Not only does the image put forward demonize veterans and group all diagnosed individuals into one homogeneous group, but the absence of trauma representations in other contexts also suggests that *only* veterans can receive this diagnosis or experience trauma, which is untrue.[25] The fact that these myths are demonstrably false and yet endure is a strange endorsement of the power of popular-culture storytelling. Hillary Chute describes comics as "an art of distillation and condensation"; as such, they are wont to erase much of the nuance of an experience as complex as trauma.[26] The remainder of this chapter is given to three case studies, each of which centers traumatized veterans and addresses their experiences from different perspectives.

Trauma as Rupture: *Hellblazer* 5 and the "Destroyed" Vet

The most common image used to discuss trauma is a "rupture." Starting with Freud, the term is used extensively throughout trauma theory to suggest the breaking apart or psychological damage that is occurring within the mind when an individual experiences something traumatic. "Rupture" pays homage to the etymological root of "trauma"—the Greek word τραῦμα ("wound"), originally used as a physical, medical term (and still used with this meaning in medical discourse today). What the word conveys most clearly is severe, lasting damage to the affected area—in this case, the mind. There are four main symptom categories for PTSD diagnosis; of the categories, patients need to show at least one symptom from each for a period longer than one month. They are as follows: intrusion symptoms (such as nightmares, flashbacks, and intense distress when exposed to a cue for the traumatic event), persistent avoidance of stimuli associated with the trauma, negative moods associated with the trauma (such as persistent negative self-belief, persistent negative emotional state, and estrangement from others), and alterations in arousal and reactivity (including hypervigilance, sleeplessness, anger, and an exaggerated startle response). The symptoms must cause "clinically significant distress or impairment in social, occupational, or other important areas of functioning" to receive a PTSD diagnosis.[27] Following these criteria, Lieutenant Frank Ross in *Hellblazer* 5 is a clear example of a PTSD patient.

The story arc of *Hellblazer* 5, "When Johnny Comes Marching Home," follows Ross, the only returning veteran from a platoon of young men who went together to Vietnam from Liberty, Iowa. Twenty years after the NLF ambush that killed most of the American soldiers, their parents are praying for their return via a cultish organization called the Resurrection Crusaders. John Constantine arrives in the small town and meets Frank, who is profoundly traumatized by his combat experience and is hated by the townspeople because he returned, while their children did not. The town's now-elderly population pray (and donate huge amounts of money) to the Resurrection Crusaders, and their sons *are* resurrected and return to the town as ghosts. As Frank's flashbacks become more severe, he believes he is back in Vietnam in 1968 and shoots many of the townspeople, including his wife. The ghost marines similarly believe that they are in Vietnam and hold the elderly townspeople at gunpoint near the gas station. At the climax of the story, Frank begins firing blindly into the headlights of a passing truck, which rolls into the gas pumps, causing an explosion that destroys the town and its residents. Constantine leaves in despair, stating that he now knows that the war "smells of gasoline."[28]

There are three distinct issues that arise from this comic when we view it through the lens of trauma: the accuracy of the representation, trauma as something that also relates to grief, and the relevance of the "smell of gasoline" as a negation of the glory narrative. Within the comic, it is in the character of Frank that we see the clearest portrayal of traumatic symptoms. Indeed, it is so clear that the writers may have taken the diagnostic criteria as their guide in designing him. When Constantine arrives in Liberty, his first stop is the gas station that Frank runs with his wife, Nancy. Prior to his arrival, Frank is slumped drunkenly in a chair, drinking whiskey from the bottle. His alcoholism is a form of self-medication to protect him from the negative emotional states that are a part of PTSD. As Constantine enters the gas station, Frank's flashbacks are placing him at the death of a young Vietnamese woman, and he misidentifies both his wife and Constantine as this woman. He is in a psychotic traumatic break and shoots at them, showing the severity of his traumatic symptoms, including hypervigilance and psychosis.

Later, Frank wakes from a nightmare, believing himself to be back in theater, and arms himself. This series of actions is paired on the page by a similar sequence happening in Vietnam. He wakes, straps on his firearms belt and holsters, and walks into the jungle—represented in Iowa as the fields of corn. In placing both events side by side, the narrative splits in two ways. First, we simultaneously see where Frank thinks he is (back in Vietnam) and where he actually is (Iowa), mimicking the experience of traumatic flashbacks and dissociation. Juxtaposing the two events—and furthermore, mirroring Frank's movements across both—shows how trauma brings the past into

BROKEN KITES 115

the present in ways that corrupt the patient's experiences and affect their engagement with their present situation. Second, if we look closer at the way the page is laid out, we see that the Vietnam-sequence panels are larger and take up more of the page. Their size shows the importance of the event in the formation of Frank's mental state and the prevalence of it in his memory. His combat experiences take up more mental space and importance than any other memory or experience. They govern his daily existence.

Frank's story ends in tragedy, as we as readers may expect from the beginning. As his trauma psychosis becomes increasingly violent, Nancy attempts to reason with him. Frank sees only the face of a Vietnamese woman he murdered, and he plays out the flashback in his brain. The scene plays out in the cornfields, which are both a site of action and a visual code for the dense vegetation and disorientation of the Vietnamese jungle—a maize maze, if you will. On the page, the interaction between Frank and Nancy is depicted in bandeau panels with very little background detail. The center of the page is divided by a large, stark, white crack. At the moment of Frank's most awful trauma-motivated act, the traumatic rupture within his brain becomes visible on the page; though he has struggled with his PTSD symptoms for nineteen years, he has now taken a life in a noncombat situation.[29] Nancy's death is not directly shown on the page. Instead, her death is represented by a burst of rifle fire ("BADDABADDA!") and the reaction of Constantine, who is hiding in the corn nearby ("Oh Christ").[30] From the point at which the page itself splinters, Frank is no longer in Iowa. He is fully in Vietnam, and the story in Liberty ends when the town is destroyed by an explosion at the gas station.

The ending is, in some ways, merciful. The entire town was suffering. Frank was exhibiting symptoms from all four categories within the DSM criteria. His actions were guided by erratic and mentally unsound decision-making. His relationships, with his wife and others, were deeply disturbing. His self-medication with alcohol was ineffective at treating the symptoms that were ruling his life. But it was not just Frank who was affected by the trauma of the events in Vietnam nineteen years previous. The entire town was consumed by grief and the loss of their sons. The older members of the community (no other members are shown, and the implication is that all the young people—and any of the community's daughters—had left) were paying into a prayer scam in the hope that a televangelist would pray their sons back to them alive. The obsession with this "prayer crusade" had taken all of their money and also driven many of them to poor mental health, as no tangible assistance or support ever arrived. Their pain remained unacknowledged and was outshone by the trauma of those who experienced the horrors of combat.

At this juncture, I should make clear that we are moving away from medical definitions of trauma as a diagnosable condition and into a definition that sees it as a cultural experience. More specifically, we are looking at the culturally defined and performative expression of mourning. Many people find it difficult to engage with those who are mourning, but for Freud the process of mourning is necessary and healthy: "We look upon any interference with it as useless or even harmful."[31] Human beings are *supposed* to mourn a death; however, to allow the events and act of mourning to consume one's entire existence is not healthy and strays into what Freud terms "melancholia." Freud defines melancholia as being the result of an unhealthy work of mourning: "The patient allows the loss to absorb him entirely. . . . He vilifies himself and expects to be cast out and punished."[32] Giving oneself entirely to the whims of a charlatan in the figure of a televangelist who will take money (and, by extension, hope) from desperate people clearly demonstrates melancholia and the sufferer's loss of self. For the people of Liberty, Iowa, their grief becomes an obsession with bringing their sons home through any means necessary and at any cost, while hating the only member of the platoon who did return—Frank Ross. The irony of naming this place "Liberty" is palpable.

There is trauma in grief when it moves from a healthy processing of loss to a pathological state of despair and emotional paralysis. It is rarely shown in narratives of the Vietnam War in any form, and especially in comics. In giving space to the families of the lost, *Hellblazer* 5 entertains the possibility of shedding light on the differences in traumatic experiences of those who are not directly involved in combat but, nevertheless, are affected by the war. This group remains largely ignored in the war narrative, as does the trauma inherent in grief. The events at Liberty end with an explosion and Constantine saying, "Before, I'd only seen the war. Now, I know how it smells. It smells of gasoline."[33] In ending this way, all honor and glory is stripped from the narrative, and all that remains in the aftermath is the smell of gasoline. Once again, Iowa is paired with the jungle, as the smell of gasoline mimics the smell of napalm. The war is brought home and remains devastating.

Hellblazer 5 recenters the war in Iowa, the heartland of the United States. The trauma comes home, along with the returned vet, and destroys entire communities. This representation leans heavily into the image of the returned vet as dangerous and prone to alcoholism, domestic abuse, and community disruption. Constantine acts as a mediator for the events in Liberty; he is British and therefore exists outside the national narrative of Vietnam that underpins the whole comic. His role is to mediate between the townsfolk and Frank, working to further the narrative and to bridge (some of) the disconnection that is plaguing the town. Ultimately, though, Constantine is unable to do anything to save the town; at the comic's conclusion, he describes the town as living with "bitterness and blind faith, with a shot of guilt... a cancer that'd been growing for a long time."[34] Trauma in *Hellblazer* 5 is a destructive force, and its power is total.

Trauma as Dis/connection: Bonding and Breakage in *Enemy Ace: War Idyll*

In the previous case study, a toxic combination of grief and traumatic psychosis leads to the (literally) explosive destruction of a whole community. Though the most common, simplified view of the traumatic condition—and certainly the one we are most familiar with in popular culture—is that it is devastating to both the individual and those around them, in simplification all nuance is lost. Frank's inability to speak about his trauma—and his community's inability (or refusal) to listen—is ultimately destructive. The trope of a soldier who is unable to connect with his community after returning home is common in literatures of war. For example, Paul Bäumer, the protagonist of *All Quiet on the Western Front*, struggles to communicate with his sister and ailing mother during a period of leave. Despite being in combat for only a short period, he has become untethered to his roots and finds more similarity with other soldiers, even though they may be the enemy.[35] Similarly, in *Apocalypse Now*, Captain Willard has re-upped and returned to Saigon;[36] he describes his experience of disconnection in grim terms: "When I was home after my first tour, it was worse. I'd wake up and there'd be nothing. I hardly said a word to my wife, until I said 'yes' to a divorce. When I was here, I wanted to be there; when I was there, all I could think of was getting back into the jungle."[37] In contrast, for Edward Mannock, an American journalist and Vietnam veteran, and Hans von Hammer in George Pratt's *Enemy Ace: War Idyll* (1990), their ability to speak about their trauma creates connection.

The character Enemy Ace (the alias of Hans von Hammer) was created by Robert Kanigher and Joe Kubert, first appearing in *Our Army at War* 151 in February 1965. He is based loosely on the figure of Manfred von Richthofen (aka the Red Baron). Von Richthofen was a fighter pilot and flying ace during the First World War, credited with over eighty aerial victories. The similarities between the two men are many. Both are of noble birth, highly decorated flying aces, and pilots of red Fokker DR1 triplanes. Von Hammer is a man of honor.[38] Though he is the "enemy," he is presented with integrity and chivalry at all times. Earlier comics show him as a brilliant tactician and skilled pilot; in a later arc, he mistakenly parachutes into the concentration camp at Dachau and is outraged to discover the ongoing genocide, whereupon he surrenders his squadron to Sergeant Rock's Easy Company.[39] The clearest difference between the two characters is that von Richthofen died at the age of twenty-five, having been shot down over France, while von Hammer survived to old age.

When *Enemy Ace: War Idyll* begins, von Hammer is daydreaming about his previous war experience. The sequence shows his bright-red triplane in the midst of a dogfight. The coloration is bold and bright, contrasting with the art style: soft, melting watercolor paintings. The lack of defined lines means that panels are visually chaotic, even when the content of the scene is a simple conversation between the two men. Elsewhere, I have argued that comics use their "arsenal of formal representational techniques to produce affect in the reader and, in doing so, [mimic] (some part of) the feelings and experience of trauma."[40] The use of visually chaotic artwork in this comic mimics the enduring nature of the trauma. In stark contrast to the watercolor images, the panel borders are distinct, with well-defined gutters. The effect is jarring—while the anarchic content of the panels mimics the trauma of the individuals, the careful order of the borders only adds to the discomfort.

Throughout *Enemy Ace: War Idyll* there is a clear distinction in the use of color to create narrative distance between reality and memory. When the two men first meet, von Hammer's hospital room is darkened, with the only light coming from the television. The artwork is extremely dark, almost exclusively black and gray, with pale-blue highlights to simulate the only light in the room. This dark coloration continues throughout the comic as the two men talk. However, in bold contrast, the artistic representation of their war memories, which are presented with a voiceover, is bright and strongly colored. This means that von Hammer's memories are rendered in sky blue, punctuated with the red of his plane and the orange of fires and gunshots. Mannock's memories of his time in the tunnels and jungles of Vietnam are rendered in equally bright coloration. Both men experience their memory of combat more vividly than reality; the memory takes on a vibrant, horrible presence in their daily existence, a symptom that many veterans with PTSD and PTS suffer.[41]

Upon their first meeting, von Hammer recognizes their common understanding when he first addresses his visitor: "Your eyes ... you didn't tell me you were a soldier, Mister Mannock. You will always be a soldier."[42] The two men talk in terms of "my war" and "your war," highlighting the difference between their combat experiences. Mannock is a young American journalist who survived his tour in Vietnam and comes from a working-class midwestern community. He has used his position as a journalist to gain access to von Hammer, though he confesses to the old man that his initial ruse of the interview being an assignment from his editor is not true.[43] Mannock seeks out von Hammer to speak to him about his experiences and to try to find some kind of relief from his trauma.

The moment of connection comes halfway through the comic. Von Hammer's war stories have opened Mannock to speaking, and so he does. During his time as a tunnel rat, his group of three were attacked by NLF soldiers in the tunnels. Acting out of pure survival instinct, Mannock shields himself behind the already-injured body of his fellow soldier. As the gunfire ceases, he crawls to safety, eventually emerging aboveground by climbing up through a mass grave of NLF soldiers. Mannock's trauma is heavily bound up in survivor guilt, and he berates himself for surviving, when his fellow soldiers did not. Cathy Caruth, after Freud, sees trauma as "not the reaction to any horrible event but, rather, the peculiar and perplexing experience of survival."[44] While survivors feel (and are told) that they should be grateful that they survived, such gratitude does not come easily, as the individual must recalibrate their understanding of their existence around what they have experienced. Here is the moment of intense connection—as Mannock tells his story and sobs, von Hammer places his hand on Mannock's bowed head. It is a gesture of connection and blessing, as well as support and paternalism. Von Hammer knows exactly what Mannock is talking about, and he understands the complex emotional response that comes with it. Even without the added layer of PTSD, survival of a life-threatening situation is an intense and deeply affecting experience. For von Hammer, they are both "cogs in the war machine," and their survival need not make sense.[45]

Enemy Ace: War Idyll stresses not only the possibility of connection for sufferers of trauma but also that trauma itself is highly individualized. Trauma as a personal and individual experience is now understood by trauma theorists and clinicians, but this has not always been the case, as already mentioned. In forging connection between two distinct individuals, this comic represents trauma as both intensely personal and also containing a common core that can generate connection and community. When veterans are denied this opportunity for community, their traumatic experience deepens into isolation. Furthermore, the comic shows trauma as something that cannot be cured. As von Hammer states, "There is no secret ... each person experiences war personally, separately. We see differently. We remember differently. You will always have your own war. You will go to bed with it and you will wake with it."[46] The trauma remains, but the individual learns to cope.

Whereas in *Hellblazer* 5 and the majority of other comics that mention vets (however briefly), trauma leads only to disconnection from one's family and community, in *Enemy Ace: War Idyll* it becomes a way to find new community and connection between two people who have very little in common. Von Hammer and Mannock bond over their mutual understanding of conflict trauma. They have previously found themselves unable to share their trauma with those who have not been through the experience. They are silenced by the community's inability and unwillingness to listen but find their voice in each other's company. The irony, of course, is that the connection is forged between an American and a German. Not only would they have been on opposite sides of the earlier conflict, but there are several generations between them. Their conflicts (and their roles within them) are vastly different in how they played out. However, as von Hammer says, "war is one of life's inevitable aberrations ... a paradox. Nothing but an endless loop of absurd contradictions. Boredom and routine punctuated by slaughter."[47]

The connection between von Hammer and Mannock enriches both of them and demonstrates the ways in which traumatic experience is not doomed to silence but can be given voice. The final case study of this chapter, *The Legion of Charlies*, also shows that creating community and connection is possible and necessary for traumatized veterans. However, in this text, the expression of community is far from positive.

Trauma as Collective: *The Legion of Charlies* Eat the Vice President

Trauma is distinctly personal and unique; no two people will experience trauma the same way. It is the acceptance of this individuality that has led to some of the most important developments in the treatment of trauma as a psychomedical condition. Since 2001 it has become increasingly common to view contemporary events through this lens, despite it not always being helpful or appropriate. For example, much of the discourse of trauma that surrounds the 2001 terrorist attack on the World Trade Center does not take into account the true nature of what trauma really is and how it manifests in a person; it would be more accurate to talk about the experience of witnessing horrible events that people could not influence, which can be deeply upsetting and emotionally affecting but is distinct from trauma. That said, when detached from the lexicon of medicalization and diagnosis, trauma is a lens through which to view collective experiences.

If we consider trauma as a representational and narratological lens for retelling the stories of soldiers' war experiences, we can navigate the tricky ethical issue of appropriating others' pain. We can consider certain events as collective trauma, and this lens can be used to understand how a group of people bond over it. Such a trauma "is shared collectively and frequently has a cohesive effect as individuals gather in small and intimate groups to reflect on the tragedy and its consequences. Personal feelings of sadness, fear, and anger are confirmed when others express similar emotions."[48] At the same time, collective trauma often gives space for the absurdity and banality of trauma to be brought to the fore, and the symptoms of trauma become acute madness. It is this acute madness that becomes the focus of Tom Veitch, Greg Irons, and Dave Sheridan's *The Legion of Charlies* (1971). For Veitch, Irons, and Sheridan, "dismissing or ignoring the traumatic experience is not a reasonable option," and the trauma experienced by returning service members becomes homicidal, cannibalistic psychosis.[49]

The comic opens with a series of parallel bandeau panels that juxtapose the Mỹ Lai massacre (March 16, 1968) and the Manson family murders (August 8–10, 1969).[50] In parallel, we see the massacre of Vietnamese civilians and the murder of Manson's victims. The final page of this short introduction shows Charles Manson strapped into an electric chair, being executed for "the unspeakable murders of America's movie stars, and for the heinous corruption of our daughters."[51] In contrast, Calley (here named "Rusty Kali") is awarded the Silver Star, "although [he] thoughtlessly snuffed the lives of 400 gook women and children."[52] One set of murders is among the most famous and heinous crimes of the twentieth century; the other is cause for celebration and medals. And though there was a trial and large-scale condemnation of the Mỹ Lai massacre, the suggestion is that many would agree with Calley's actions. The tone for the comic as a whole is set. No part of it is subtle, and the critique of the U.S. military, and the war more broadly, permeates every page. Though Calley, or Kali, is positioned as a puppet of circumstance and of the government, he is also viewed as culpable in his own right.

The body of the narrative follows Kali after his release from prison. He visits San Francisco and solicits a sex worker, whom he later murders during sex; it is implied that his violent murderous outburst is triggered by an intense and disturbing sexual attraction to violence, which is caused by his actions in Mỹ Lai.

Kali takes psychedelic drugs and has a vision of Charles Manson; he becomes a "dedicated follower of the word of Charlie!"[53] Simultaneously, hundreds of other Vietnam veterans across the country undergo the same transformation, inciting a mass migration of zombified veterans to the mountains of Utah, where the Legion of Charlies is born. The group are invited to Washington DC, where they kidnap and eat Spiro Agnew, before taking off around the world, eating political leaders to assume their powers. In the final pages, the Charlies meet with President Nixon, who attempts to steal the Charlies' accumulated power before a lightning strike sent by Manson (from the heavens) kills the president and his bodyguards.

For Kali and the Legion of Charlies, their trauma is a collective-bonding thread that links them and that acts like psychical programming (in a *Manchurian Candidate* way) to be activated by the "word of Charlie." The experience of trauma itself can create a bond. Because of the way that soldiers were cycled in and out of platoons according to their individual tour of duty, they were not necessarily from similar geographic areas, and so the return home was often an intensely isolating experience, as we have previously seen in *Hellblazer* 5.

It is, of course, highly unlikely that groups of traumatized veterans would march on Washington DC and eat the vice president. The vast majority of vets were a danger only to themselves.[54] *The Legion of Charlies* is, instead, "a gruesome parable of violence in America and how the government's endorsement of ruthless killing parallels the vile madness of an incorrigible murderer."[55] Defenders of Calley, or Kali, may use the old excuse of "just following orders," but that is not an excuse here.[56] His actions are markedly different from those of Charles Manson, but both led groups that committed horrific acts of violence against innocent people. What *The Legion of Charlies* makes most evident is that—for Veitch, Irons, and Sheridan—Calley is a representative of "the millions of young men whose minds have been (and continue to be) corrupted for the purpose of carrying out government agendas."[57]

Conclusion

After the Fall

> You can kill ten of my men for every one I kill of yours. But even at those odds, you will lose and I will win.
> —HO CHI MINH (1946)

The United States of America is a country born of violence and one that exists in a state of perpetual violent re-creation. I write this in 2024; in the 248 years since the country's founding, there have been only seventeen years of peace. Among these decades of conflict are wars of all sizes and for all reasons. The United States has fought alone and with others. It has joined fights along ideological lines, and it has fought territorial battles to retain—or to steal—land. Its military is the largest in the world by a wide margin. Current data shows that "the United States now spends more on defense than the next 10 countries combined."[1] Among all this conflict and violence, the Vietnam War is unique—in its lack of fronts, its guerrilla nature, and its outcome, which remains contested. It is also, as mentioned previously, the first television war.[2]

Journalists were embedded within the military to see the war up close. The narrative that was being broadcast into American homes nightly was in the hands of the media. The result was an imaginary of the war that was very much bound up in sensationalist television reportage. Neil Postman writes that "entertainment is the supra-ideology of television."[3] What was being broadcast was what the television audiences wanted to see—American soldiers fighting and winning. And this focus was not solely an issue for televisual news coverage, though the televisual presence of the war has a clear impact on its popular-culture rendering. As I have demonstrated throughout this book, the erasures and silencing of other voices within the war narrative has impacted comics.

American mythogenesis of the war has created a visual narrative and a rich iconography that has skewed the national narrative to the point that certain groups no longer feature, and the war becomes one of white American masculinity. The vast majority of representations of the war in popular culture—be they cinematic, televisual, literary, or comics—recenter the U.S. narrative. Furthermore, the narrative being put forward in American cultural artifacts—visual, written, or aural—is necessarily affected by misinformation and skewed understandings of events. The fact that so many voices are excluded from the stories that make up the prevailing narrative only heightens this skewing. A narrative that ignores so many of an event's players cannot be accurate.

This is not to say that the Vietnamese never put forward a compelling narrative; they were very successful in promoting their political stance during the war, both on the international stage and within the United States. The majority of material support came from China and the Soviet Union. China lists its aid total as $20 billion, including five million tons of food.[4] Similarly, the Soviet Union sent large amounts of support, especially military hardware, totaling $450 million.[5] They also sent eleven thousand service personnel, and it is thanks to the KGB that the North Vietnamese had signal-intelligence capabilities.[6] But this does *not* translate into comics. The intervention and assistance of other nations on both sides of the conflict is not unknown within the historiography of the war, but it has not massively affected the mononarrative of the war that is still being rolled out in popular-culture representations.

There are other voices, but their opportunity to be heard is limited. For many, it is due to translation. There is a small but powerful body of literature within Vietnam (and in Vietnamese) that gives voice to this side of the conflict. Probably the most well-known novel is *The Sorrow of War*, by Bảo Ninh (1991); translated into English in 1993. Much of the nontranslated corpus is overtly political and speaks to the successes of the NLF. American poet John Balaban collected a huge amount of sung oral poetry and translated it, publishing *Ca Dao Việt Nam: Vietnamese Folk Poetry* in 1980. Balaban's work brought Vietnamese-language work to U.S. readers but remains in the margin of the war's narrative; the dominant narrative remains Americentric.

Throughout this book, I have demonstrated the ways in which comics have played into the construction of the narrative and national myth of the Vietnam War; I have repeatedly highlighted the silence of marginalized voices, the ways in which the war is represented as an American conflict, and the issues that arise from this presentation. The corpus of comics I have discussed represents a cross section of American-created and American-published texts from the early 1950s to the present day. In the previous chapters—which discuss the Vietnamese, women, and returning vets—I have demonstrated how these three groups are largely ignored in the hegemonic narrative of the Vietnam War. This being said, there are two texts that stand in opposition to the rest of the corpus. Their existence complicates the narrative by representing voices we do not find elsewhere and demonstrating the possibilities for telling these missing stories.

Listening to the Other Side: Two Views from Vietnam

If one were to pick up either GB Tran's *Vietnamerica* or Thi Bui's *The Best We Could Do* expecting a vibrant war narrative, with bombs and detailed interactions between hard-boiled military personnel, they would be disappointed. These two comics are not war comics, at least not in the sense that we may think. These two texts present an ethnographic corrective to the common Americentric comic of Vietnam. These comics are snapshots of the immediate moment, of the military task at hand. What Tran and Bui construct, in sharp contrast, is a multigenerational family saga, weaving their present-day experiences of life in the United States with their parents' and grandparents' histories, stretching back to the French colonial presence in Vietnam and the twenty-year span of the conflict. The war is not simply one event among many; it is an ongoing narrative of colonial oppression and international intervention, with specific and targeted effects on those involved. For Tran and Bui, the Vietnam War is not *just* a military interaction between national players that occurred between 1955 and 1975. It is part of the enduring history of their family's home and their own personal identity construction. Both texts foreground the experiences of those whom I have previously described as silenced: the Vietnamese (both soldiers and civilians), women, and those who were traumatized by their war experiences. The comics' space becomes the battlefield for their retelling of this new Vietnamese-centric narrative. These texts do not replace the classic narrative of Vietnam, but they sit alongside it, to offer a counternarrative to the one put in place by American mythmakers, rounding out the characters and ensuring that the true struggles of the Vietnamese—and their own stories of the war—are not lost.

Vietnamerica opens with an image of a plane traversing a

bright-red sky, above Saigon. A disembodied voice says, "You know what your father was doing at your age? He . . . WE left Vietnam."[7] The first page of the text—indeed, the very first words—sets up a disjunction between generations and gives us the primary theme of the text: family histories and identity construction. The speaker is Tran's mother, Dzung, speaking as the family returns to Vietnam to visit; this is GB's first trip to his parents' homeland. Kaus writes that "through this interplay between word and image, GB is able to span two temporal periods in one instance, juxtaposing them to emphasize the necessity of telling the past, which, though past, remains present."[8] The decision to start this book by talking about departures and endings, despite it being in tandem with an arrival, is a curious one. Caroline Hong writes, "The nonlinear structure . . . depicting GB's trip narratively before his parents' much earlier return, serves to close the gap between the two trips and render the timeline of these histories less important than their parallel nature. Rather than emphasize chronology and hierarchy, Tran creates a genealogy that highlights shared experiences across generations, something unimaginable to GB prior to his journey."[9] The family experience is the thing; for Tran this text is an important intervention into his personal history and a document of overcoming. It has been for *him*, rather than his parents, to overcome their past and understand its relationship to him. His return to Vietnam is essential for this overcoming, because it gives location to his history.

Tran, born in the United States after his family's migration from Vietnam in 1975, sees himself as a person of fragmented identity. However, the act of telling the story of his family and their movement through French- and American-occupied Vietnam, to the Philippines, and finally to the United States, becomes an act of remembering. As Kaus writes, "graphic memoirs make it clear that their narratives are reconstructions but not reflections of the past. Viewers must acknowledge that they offer not objective authenticity but subjective accounting."[10] Tran is not telling his parents' story as a clear and historical narrative; he is telling his parents' story as it relates both to him directly and to the wider conflict. What does the constantly shifting sociopolitical situation in Vietnam mean for his family, and furthermore, how do they develop within it?

In contrast to American-born Tran, Thi Bui was born in Saigon and spent her first three years in Vietnam before her family left for the United States, via a refugee camp in Malaysia. Bui opens her book with a detailed and often-graphic description of the birth of her son. She uses this narrative of birth and creation to introduce the theme of family, which runs through her work, similar to Tran's story. Both she and Tran position their parents as central figures in their own identity-construction narratives, and both consider the impact of their parents' traumatization on their own upbringing. Throughout *The Best We Could Do*, Bui places family landmarks and conflict landmarks in close contrast. Her sister, Bich, was born in January 1968, and "two weeks later the Tet Offensive began." Her brother, Tam, was born in 1978 in the Malaysian refugee camp. Bui herself was born only a few months before the fall of Saigon.[11] In closely juxtaposing births and conflict events (which it would not be a stretch to conflate with deaths) on the page—often in adjoining or overlapping panels—Bui maps her own history onto the wider history of the country. Her family is breaking and remaking itself as the country does the same. The mentioned conflict events received massive amounts of news coverage internationally, with nightly updates being broadcast on American television news. The numbers of servicemen killed in action was of interest; the number of babies born into conflict was not—the invisible counterwar, existing in parallel and in silence.

Both *Vietnamerica* and *The Best We Could Do* are populated almost entirely by Vietnamese characters. The few exceptions are American soldiers with limited interactions within the story. *Vietnamerica* gives detailed and rich descriptions of Vietnam during the French colonial occupation and explanations of the development of the Vietnamese Communist Party, the Việt Minh, and the NLF. The complexity of these histories, and of Tran's relationship to them, is stark and most clearly expressed in the figure of Huu Nghiep, his paternal grandfather. Tran's father, Tri, and his father are estranged. Tri does not remember him fondly, and Huu Nghiep is depicted as a stern and cold figure who did not care for his family. However, in a scene where Tri and GB visit Huu Nghiep's widow, this opinion is called into question. A painting displayed prominently is later revealed to be by Tri; unknown by him, it was bought by Huu Nghiep at Tri's first exhibition. Though the hint is small, the prominence of the work within Huu Nghiep's home does not suggest as unsympathetic a character as Tri would have us believe. Huu Nghiep is representative of the political situation in Vietnam and the tearing of loyalties that occur in wartime: on the one hand, a brave war hero and loyal member of the Communist party and, on the other, a man of wavering family allegiance.

As I have previously discussed, *The Best We Could Do* brings together the landmarks of international and of familial history. But Bui does not shy away from challenging the classic view of the Vietnam War and of the Vietnamese. Her father speaks of General Loan, made infamous in Eddie Adams's 1968 photograph *Saigon Execution*, with ambiguity, leaving Thi trying to decide whether or not her father supported the general's actions. These contradictions trouble her, but "so did the oversimplifications and stereotypes in American versions" of the war.[12] She sees the stereotypes as being in three distinct groups: the "good guys" (the Americans), the "bad guys" (the Viet Cong, who are "very hard to see"), and the "South Vietnamese" (encompassing "bar girls and hookers, corrupt leaders, small, effete men and papa-san").[13] You are, I hope, aware of the nuance and enormous complexity of the conflict by this point in the text and that these three categories appear at best laughably naive, at worst offensive and culturally insensitive. Bui outlines the different version of the story of "that day, April 30, 1975."[14] Bui describes the "American version" as "one of South Vietnamese cowardice, corruption, and ineptitude . . . South Vietnamese soldiers abandoning their uniforms in the stress . . . Americans crying at their wasted efforts to save a country not worth saving. But Communist forces entered Saigon without a fight, and no blood was shed."[15] Whereas Tran's subversion of the classic narrative is bound up in the existence of the book itself—the fact it exists is enough to be a statement against the classic narrative—Bui goes one step further and makes it explicit. Not only does she clearly outline the stereotypes, highlighting their true nature, but she clarifies the multivalent story of the fall of Saigon, which became bound up in Hubert van Es's photograph *22 Gia Long Street* and the retreat narrative put forward by the United States.

In the Americentric view, April 1975 signaled the end of the war. Tran and Bui know that this is most certainly not the case and that the war lives on in their experiences and family histories, in their understanding of certain pieces of their culture, and in the homes they make for their children. Bui describes the conflict as a chessboard—a "game of war and strategy." She writes, "My grandparents, my parents, my sisters, and me—we weren't any of the pieces on the chessboard."[16] For her, as for Tran, the conflict extends long beyond the fall of Saigon, as both families struggled to rebuild and relocate, managing their identities as both exemplar refugees and nuanced individuals. Tran uses a similar board game visual metaphor, this time using

Scrabble, to represent the struggles the family has faced in relocating to the United States and acclimating to a markedly different culture. In one double-page image, a Scrabble board is laid out, with words including "threatening," "culture," and "foreign."[17] To the side of the board, "four letters forming 'home' appear un-played beside the board, indicative of the feeling of homelessness prevalent throughout the refugees' experiences."[18] Scrabble is used throughout Tran's story; he is shown playing the game with his grandmother and his older sister, both during intense conversations about family and identity.[19]

These two parallel metaphors are representative of the ability of the comics form to reinvigorate existing narrative techniques. In creating a narrative palimpsest on the board games, itself a form of entertainment recognized across cultural divides, both artists are able to convey large swathes of individual personal histories that may be alien to the reader, while framing the narratives themselves in an object that is recognizable to the reader. The board game frame acts as a cultural leveler, while standing as an excellent example of the power of comics to represent the often-intangible nuance of individual histories. As Edward Said claims, "Comics seemed to say what couldn't otherwise be said, perhaps what wasn't permitted to be said or imagined, defying the ordinary processes of thought, which are policed, shaped and re-shaped by all sorts of pedagogical as well as ideological pressures.... I felt that comics free me to think and imagine and see differently."[20] Both Tran and Bui are taking a narrative that we assume we know well—the classic Vietnam War story—and drastically reframing it. A story of intervention, militarism, and heroism becomes one of invasion, family struggle, and reclamation of national histories.

Viet Thanh Nguyen describes "the industry of memory" as incorporating "the processes of individual memory, the collective nature of its making, and the social contexts of its meanings."[21] The American industry of Vietnam memory is manufacturing a memory of the war that considers only small portions of the social contexts. He further suggests that this removal of the Vietnamese from their own stories is proof that "wealthy and powerful countries can export their memories more effectively than poorer ones."[22] The Vietnamese American industry, as exemplified in Tran and Bui, brings in the portion that the classic narrative excludes. Ultimately, both Tran and Bui are using their texts to reclaim their history, and their comics exist in difficult relationship to the wider corpus of American comics of the war. They give voice to characters that are otherwise silent in other comics; their representation of the conflict is nuanced and speaks to the multigenerational and intensely complex geopolitical struggle. These comics dissolve the traditional boundaries of "battlefield" and "hearth" to place the war directly into the lives of all those who experienced it, combatant or civilian. They were written by artists who had a direct, family connection to the conflict. This history is *their* history, and this is their story.

For the rest of the corpus, which erases and silences, it is not simply that these voices are ignored. It is not just that the story being told is not theirs, but it is a completely different story to begin with. The task at hand is not to write a Vietnam story and erase the Vietnamese but to write a proper American Vietnam War story. The material that goes into building this narrative is from the decades of American mythogenesis that places American servicemen at the center of the war narrative, which excludes all voices that add layers of complexity and complication and which clearly demonstrates that, though the United States did *not* win the war in Vietnam, they have undoubtedly won the war of representation, at least on the American comics market. The Vietnam War *can* accommodate a multiplicity of voices and narratives, which enrich the overall story of the war and give space to the many disparate experiences that go into any multinational conflict event. The war is big enough to accommodate all these voices. All have a place in creating the event that we (more precisely, some of us) call the Vietnam War.

NOTES

SERIES EDITORS' INTRODUCTION

1. Although the U.S. Armed Forces have been actively deployed in combat zones throughout the period since, the nation's most recent official declaration of war took place on June 4, 1942.

INTRODUCTION

Epigraph: Apple, "McNamara Recalls, and Regrets, Vietnam," 12.

1. Calverton, "Cultural Barometer," 101.
2. Lund, "Rethinking the Jewish–Comics Connection," 7.
3. Nye, *Bound to Lead*, 166.
4. We may see this as being related to Bourdieu's concept of "symbolic violence," which "is violence perpetrated on us through tacit consent on the part of those who fall victim to it and also, often, on the part of those who use it, if both do not perceive at all that they use violence or suffer from it." Bourdieu, *Language and Symbolic Power*, 41. The true power of symbolic violence is in its lack of perceived threat; people act voluntarily in ways they perceive to be "natural" to them, unaware that such dynamics are the result of control and symbolic violence.
5. Babiracki, *Soviet Soft Power in Poland*.
6. Seymour, "Problem with Soft Power."
7. Manor and Golan, "Irrelevance of Soft Power."
8. Dittmar and Michaud, *From Hanoi to Hollywood*, 1.
9. Other suggestions include December 1956, when the NLF insurgency in South Vietnam began; September 26, 1959, when the NLF and ARVN first met in battle; and March 8, 1965, when the U.S. Marines landed at Da Nang.
10. Rifas, *Korean War Comic Books*.
11. Rifas, *Korean War Comic Books*, 18.
12. Following the objections of a small number of American politicians and journalists—and the subsequent publication of Fredric

Wertham's *Seduction of the Innocent* (1954)—the call for censorship regulations for comics grew, mostly driven by fears of juvenile delinquency. In 1954 a U.S. Senate investigation led to the subsequent creation of the Comic Magazine Association of America (CMAA) and the Comics Code Authority (CCA). Only comics that bore the CCA stamp were allowed to be sold. The harsh regulations killed off the horror genre, leading to the revitalization of the superhero genre into its Silver Age (1956–c. 1970). To a twenty-first-century reader, the regulations of the CCA seem, at best, strict or, at worst, hilarious. Although the CCA has not been used since 2011—and no longer has any power over which comics are published and distributed in the United States—at the time, it brought the comics industry to its knees and was responsible for several companies going out of business.

13. Huxley, "'Real Thing,'" 164.
14. Wagner, "Parade of Pleasure," 94, quoted in Huxley, "'Real Thing,'" 164.
15. Rifas, *Korean War Comic Books*, 185.
16. "Raiders' Roost."
17. Dower, *War without Mercy*, 10.
18. "Indo-China Raid."
19. Huxley, "Naked Aggression," 97.
20. Wright, *Comic Book Nation*, 189–90.
21. "Figure That Matters."
22. "Star-Studded Blockbuster."
23. "New Kind of War."
24. Mandelbaum, "Vietnam."
25. Cooke, *Comic Book Artist*, 3.
26. Earle, "Conflict Then; Trauma Now," 161.
27. Goodwin et al., *Blazing Combat*, 191.
28. Lawrence, *Vietnam War*, 118.
29. "Dove" is used for someone who opposes the use of the military to resolve conflict; "hawk" refers to someone who favors war. Both terms were used prior to Vietnam, but their use became more common after 1962.
30. "Somebody Turn Him Off!"
31. Reitberger and Fuchs, *Comics*, 15.
32. Nguyen, *Nothing Ever Dies*, 312.
33. Dittmar and Michaud, *From Hanoi to Hollywood*, 6–7.

34. I say "substantial" because there is a third, *In-Country Nam*, but it ran for only four issues in 1986. The comic was published by Survival Art Press and created by Tom Lewis and Ronald Ledwell. While it was an available comic about the war that concentrated solely on it, the very short run and relative obscurity means the readership is limited and the space for narrative and character development is limited. Therefore, I do not consider it to be "substantial" in the way that *The 'Nam* and *Vietnam Journal* are.
35. D. R. Epstein, "Don Lomax's Vietnam Memories."
36. Earle, *Comics, Trauma, and the New Art of War*, 125.
37. Murray, "Interview with Brian Jacks."
38. Murray, "Interview with Brian Jacks."
39. Kodosky, "Holy Tet Westy!," 1049.
40. Kodosky, "Holy Tet Westy!," 1057.
41. "Back in the Real World."
42. *Punisher Invades The 'Nam*, nos. 52–53; *Punisher Invades The 'Nam*, nos. 67–69.
43. Di Paolo, *War, Politics and Superheroes*, 116.
44. Ennis and Parlov, *Fury: My War Gone By*.
45. Eisner, *Last Day in Vietnam*.
46. The four students who died were Allison Beth Krause (aged nineteen), Jeffrey Glenn Miller (aged twenty), Sandra Lee Scheuer (aged twenty), and William Knox Schroeder (aged nineteen).
47. Earle, "How Do Comics Engage with the Vietnam War?"
48. Backderf, "'My Claim to Fame Is Footnotes,'" 283.
49. Nguyen, "Industries of Memory," 311.
50. Foucault, *History of Sexuality*, 27.
51. Foucault, *History of Sexuality*, 27.
52. Biguenet, *Silence*, 96.
53. Melville, *Bartleby, the Scrivener*.
54. Solomon, *War Made Invisible*, 15.
55. Solomon, *War Made Invisible*, 20.
56. Solomon, *War Made Invisible*, 20.
57. E. J. Epstein, *Between Fact and Fiction*, 217.
58. Lobe, "Three Major Networks."
59. Beattie, *Scar That Binds*, 105.
60. James and Berg, "College Course File," 71.
61. Spivak, "Can the Subaltern Speak?," 1988.
62. Anderson, *Columbia Guide to the Vietnam War*, 3.

63. Thu Qyunh Dong, in conversation with the author, February 12, 2023.

1. VISUALIZING THE VIETNAMESE

1. Soper, *We Go Pogo*, 39.
2. Altoff, *Oliver Hazard Perry and the Battle of Lake Erie*, 14.
3. Gould, "Ecological Costs of Militarization."
4. Frank and Melville, "Enemy Image and the Process of Change."
5. Marchetti, *Romance and the "Yellow Peril,"* 2.
6. Dower, *War without Mercy*, 156.
7. A queue is a long braid worn by Chinese men. It was compulsory during the Qing dynasty (1636–1911).
8. Hall, "Wasp's Troublesome Children," 42.
9. Xing, *Asian America through the Lens*, 55.
10. Benitez-Garcia, Nakamura, and Kaneko, "Analysis of Differences."
11. Darwin, *Expression of the Emotions in Man and Animal*, quoted in Benitez-Garcia, Nakamura, and Kaneko, "Analysis of Differences."
12. The focus here is on the comparison of Caucasian and Southeast Asian as this is the visual comparison most evident in my comics corpus. Though African American troops were also deployed in Vietnam, their appearance in these comics is rarer, though not to their outright exclusion. Additionally, the research available uses the broad terms "Southeast Asian" and "Caucasian," avoiding or erasing the nuances of specific regional anatomical difference.
13. Liew, Chan, and Rogers, "Consensus on Changing Trends," 195.
14. Liew, Chan, and Rogers, "Consensus on Changing Trends."
15. Hung and Pak, "Impact of Environment," 52.
16. "Happy Hunting Ground," 32.
17. Dower, *War without Mercy*, 10.
18. Dower, *War without Mercy*, 10.
19. Caniff, "How to Spot a Jap."
20. Austin and Hamilton, *All New, All Different?*, 39.
21. Hirsch, *Pulp Empire*, 38.
22. Hirsch, *Pulp Empire*, 38.
23. Vuorinen, *Enemy Images in War Propaganda*, 5.
24. Vuorinen, *Enemy Images in War Propaganda*, 5.
25. Frank and Melville, "Enemy Image and the Process of Change," 201.
26. Staszak, "Other/Otherness," 43.
27. Beard, "How Can You Not Shout?"
28. Vuorinen, *Enemy Images in War Propaganda*, 3.

29. Turse, *Kill Anything That Moves*, 10.
30. Turse, *Kill Anything That Moves*, 28.
31. Turse, *Kill Anything That Moves*, 50.
32. Delano and Ridgway, *Hellblazer*, 4.
33. Goscha, *Vietnam*.
34. For a detailed history of Vietnam, see Keith Weller Taylor, *The Birth of Vietnam*.
35. *Ethnic Groups in Vietnam*. These statistics are taken from the 2009 Vietnam census. However, there has been only minimal change in ethnic divisions within the population since the first census in 1979.
36. A similar problem occurred in World War II comics, as the actual combatants on different sides may not have looked very different in practice. However, they wore visibly different uniforms that clearly and quickly differentiated them (and German soldiers are overwhelmingly depicted as blond). For PAVN and ARVN soldiers, a similar tactic can be used, and these characters are shown in uniform. But this does not work for NLF and other guerrillas, or civilians, who wore no distinct uniform.
37. Huxley, "Naked Aggression," 104.
38. Huxley, "Naked Aggression," 104.
39. "Raiders' Roost," 30–36.
40. "Dien Bien Phu!," 3.
41. Kurtzman and Gaines, *Complete EC Library*, 4.
42. Rifas, "Cold War Comics," 3.
43. Rifas, "Cold War Comics," 4.
44. Rifas, "Cold War Comics," 4.
45. Dower, *War without Mercy*, 176.
46. Wright, *Comic Book Nation*, 189.
47. "Requiem for a Red," 4.
48. Wright, *Comic Book Nation*, 191.
49. "A Walk in the Sun," 11.
50. Wright, *Comic Book Nation*, 191.
51. "A Walk in the Sun," 18.
52. See the cover images of *Sarge Steel* 5 (1965) and *War Heroes* 24 (1963) for clear examples.
53. "Iron Man Is Born!" This comic includes the first mention of Iron Man. Designed by Jack Kirby, the original character is largely unrecognizable from the version commonly seen in the twenty-first century. In the first issue, he looked like a golem made of sheet metal.

54. "Captured in Vietnam!"
55. "Happy Hunting Ground," 31.
56. "Happy Hunting Ground."
57. Chireau, "White or Indian?," 197.
58. "Happy Hunting Ground," 33.
59. Kubert and Kanigher, *Our Fighting Forces*, no. 105.
60. The *áo bà ba* is a traditional Vietnamese garment, usually made from silk. The word *áo* simply means "shirt." This garment was called "black pajamas" by the U.S. troops. The *nón lá* is a conical straw hat, common throughout Southeast Asia.
61. *Super Green Beret*, no. 1. Lightning lasted for only one year and in that time published two titles: *Super Green Beret* (two issues) and *Fatman the Human Flying Saucer* (three issues).
62. Meyer Both College of Commercial Art, *Success in Commercial Art*, 6.
63. Guy Lawley, in conversation with the author, April 13, 2021.
64. See Smith, "4 Colorism."
65. Wright, *Comic Book Nation*, 189.
66. "The Good Old Days," 5.
67. "The Good Old Days," 8.
68. "The Good Old Days," 21.
69. "The Good Old Days," 12.
70. "The Good Old Days," 4.
71. Young, "There Is Nothing Grittier," 78.
72. I could assume that most people would know the name Hồ Chí Minh ("Uncle Ho"), and many would be familiar with Võ Nguyên Giáp and Ngô Đình Diệm. However, these are not commonly known names among Americans and certainly not comparable to figures from World War II.
73. Grell, *Jon Sable, Freelance*, 24.
74. Thai, *Insufficient Funds*, 79.
75. Thai, *Insufficient Funds*, 79.
76. Loan was not the only prominent South Vietnamese figure to move to the United States in exile. The former prime minister of South Vietnam Nguyễn Cao Kỳ fled after the fall of Saigon in April 1975 and eventually opened a liquor store in California.
77. Salaita, "Beyond Orientalism and Islamophobia," 246.
78. Kakihara, "Post-9/11 Paradigm Shift," 5.
79. Kakihara, "Post-9/11 Paradigm Shift," 5.

80. Despite their publication order, *Punisher: The Platoon* is the first half of the origin story, while *The Punisher: Born* is the latter half. I discuss them here in narrative order.
81. Ennis and Parlov, *Punisher: The Platoon*.
82. Ennis and Parlov, *Punisher: The Platoon*.
83. Firebase Valley Forge is similar to the Do Lung Bridge scene in *Apocalypse Now* (1979), as both are close to Cambodia and long forgotten by central command. This type of setting has become a common trope in Vietnam narratives, carrying heavy symbolic weight for the feelings of psychological and emotional abandonment felt by many troops, as well as the increasing lack of concern seemingly felt by commanding officers.
84. Bandeau panels are those that span the full width of the page.
85. Hill and Ciaramella, *Cape*, 36.
86. Fellman, *Japanese Tattoo*; Jahnke and Jahnke, "Politics of Māori Image and Design."
87. Hasford's novel formed the basis of the film *Full Metal Jacket* (1987); he is also known for his theft of nearly eight hundred library books from several American libraries throughout the 1980s, which led to a prison sentence and a hefty fine.
88. Richards, "Descent into Hell."
89. Aaron and Stewart, *Other Side*, 54.
90. Aaron and Stewart, *Other Side*, 10–11.
91. Aaron and Stewart, *Other Side*, 13.

2. FROM ROUND-EYE TO SNIPER SPY

1. Kubrick, *Full Metal Jacket*.
2. The only other female character in the film is also unnamed. Despite her significant role in the film's climax, she is listed only as "VC Sniper." The two characters are played by Papillon Soo Soo and Ngoc Le, respectively.
3. Nguyen, "From Colonialism to Covid."
4. Stur, *Beyond Combat*, 79.
5. Stur, *Beyond Combat*, 79.
6. American women who are represented in these comics are overwhelmingly white.
7. See Elshtain, *Women and War*; Cook, *Women and War*.
8. Holmes, *Oxford Companion to Military History*, 170.
9. Stur, *Beyond Combat*, 108.

10. Stur, *Beyond Combat*, 46.
11. Taylor, *Vietnamese Women at War*.
12. Jeffords, *Remasculinization of America*.
13. Slotkin, *Regeneration through Violence*, 19.
14. Guillemot, "Death and Suffering at First Hand," 46.
15. Brox, *Silence*, 173.
16. Brox, *Silence*, 174.
17. Brownmiller, *Against Our Will*, 32.
18. Brownmiller, *Against Our Will*, 32.
19. Weaver, *Ideologies of Forgetting*, xiv.
20. Brownmiller, *Against Our Will*.
21. Orrin C. Judd, "distant and derivative," November 30, 2000, Amazon online review of Larry Heinemann, *Paco's Story: A Novel*, Vintage Contemporaries ed. (New York: Vintage Books, 1987), https://www.amazon.com/gp/customer-reviews/R1C6SHY3HL5OX6/ref=cm_cr_getr_d_rvw_ttl?ie=UTF8&ASIN=1400076838.
22. Weaver, *Ideologies of Forgetting*, 124.
23. See Brownmiller, *Against Our Will*; MacKinnon, *Feminism Unmodified*.
24. Ahrens, "Being Silenced," 263.
25. Ahrens, "Being Silenced," 263.
26. Kleinman, "Silence Is the Language of Rape."
27. Lomax, "Cordon and Search."
28. Lomax, "Cordon and Search."
29. Lomax, "Cordon and Search."
30. Lomax, "Cordon and Search."
31. Brownmiller, *Against Our Will*, 88.
32. Ennis, Robertson, and Palmer, *Punisher: Born*.
33. Ennis, Robertson, and Palmer, *Punisher: Born*.
34. Kodosky, "Holy Tet Westy!," 117.
35. Davis, *Prostitution*, 334.
36. Randal, "Nhatrang Fights Vice 'Grottoes.'"
37. Gilkes, "Missing from History."
38. Hayslip, *When Heaven and Earth Changed Places*, 293.
39. Gustafsson, "'Freedom. Money. Fun. Love.,'" 312.
40. Gustafsson, "'Freedom. Money. Fun. Love.,'" 320.
41. See Gustafsson, "'Freedom. Money. Fun. Love.': The Warlore of Vietnamese Bargirls" (2011); Park, *Narratives of the Vietnam War by Korean and American Writers* (2007); Moe, *The Vietnam Whore* (2019).

42. "Three Day Pass," 15.
43. See Earle, *Comics, Trauma, and the New Art of War*, 85–88, for an analysis of this dream sequence.
44. Phil and Nick Hunter are the sons of Lieutenant Ben Hunter, who features in several World War II story arcs in the same series.
45. "Kewpie" is a brand of doll, first manufactured in the United States in 1912. The dolls are plump, cherubic babies with a blonde curl of hair and a love heart detail on the chest, which bears the word "Kewpie."
46. Kubert, Kanigher, and Abel, *Our Fighting Forces*, no. 100, 10.
47. Lomax, "Birds of Prey." "Boom-boom" is a common slang term for sex, used by Vietnamese sex workers. The PX (i.e., Post Exchange) is a store on U.S military installations for use by soldiers.
48. Lomax, "Birds of Prey."
49. Leonard Rifas to the author, November 11, 2023.
50. Senate Committee on the Judiciary, Comic Books and Juvenile Delinquency, *Code of the Comics Magazine Association of America, Inc.*
51. Murray and Heath, *Hearts and Minds*.
52. Berger, *Ways of Seeing*, 45.
53. Berger, *Ways of Seeing*, 46.
54. Murray and Heath, *Hearts and Minds*.
55. Murray and Heath, *Hearts and Minds*.
56. Nguyen, "From Colonialism to Covid."
57. Though the term "combatant" may be used to include all those who work for the war in some way, including auxiliary staff, in this context I refer to women in active combat roles.
58. The full range of military roles was opened to women in 2016.
59. S. C. Taylor, *Vietnamese Women at War*.
60. For detailed discussions of Vietnamese women in combat, see S. C. Taylor, *Vietnamese Women at War*; Turner-Gottschang and Phan, *Even the Women Must Fight*.
61. S. C. Taylor, *Vietnamese Women at War*.
62. Turley, "Women in the Communist Revolution in Vietnam," 793.
63. Turley, "Women in the Communist Revolution in Vietnam," 803.
64. Su, "Women of the Vietnam War."
65. Keith Weller Taylor, *Birth of Vietnam*, 41.
66. Aaron and Stewart, *Other Side*, 54.
67. Alighieri, *The Inferno*, 23. This quotation is from canto 3, lines 1–3.
68. At this point, I should say that women are often positioned as snipers, rather than "normal" soldiers. Unlike male representations of

the sniper—depicted as highly trained, incredibly powerful specialist soldiers and sharpshooters—women snipers are shown as insidious killers who ignore the rules of good sportsmanship to sneak and skulk. The female sniper is similar to the poisoner. Poisoning is among the most common methods of murder chosen by women; it is similarly sneaky and favors access over strength. Women tend to poison because they have access to the victims and their food; snipers must be small and quiet, rather than strong and powerful.

69. It is, however, an ugly foreshadowing of Castle's motivations for becoming the Punisher in the years after his Vietnam tours. According to the Marvel Comics canon, Castle becomes the Punisher, a vigilante aiming to bring down organized crime in New York City, following the murder of his wife and two children by the mob. This origin story was first featured in *Marvel Preview* 2 (July 1975).
70. Race, *War Comes to Long An*.
71. Turner-Gottschang and Phan, *Even the Women Must Fight*, 28.
72. Landivar, *Men in Nursing Occupations*, 3; United Nations, *World's Women*, 82.
73. Thomas, Kang, and Dalager, "Mortality among Women Vietnam Veterans," 974.
74. Vuic, *Officer, Nurse, Woman*, 41.
75. Stur, *Beyond Combat*, 106.
76. This is not the first time this series was renamed. It began in 1955 as *Brenda Starr* before becoming *Young Lovers* (issue 16) in May 1957 and then *My Secret Life* (issue 19) in August 1957. It was marketed as a romance comic for young women and girls; the Sue and Sally Smith story in issue 47 was the first to include any themes of war or nursing.
77. Lomax, "Dustoff."

3. BROKEN KITES

1. Vonnegut, *Slaughterhouse-Five*, 70.
2. Aristotle, *Politics*, 23.
3. O'Brien, *Things They Carried*, 80.
4. Appy, *American Reckoning*, 239.
5. Appy, *American Reckoning*, 248.
6. Appy, *American Reckoning*, 248.
7. There is a considerable body of research that demonstrates that those suffering with serious mental illness, including PTSD, are less likely than the general population to engage in violence. They are,

however, more likely to be victims of violent crime. See Choe, Teplin, and Abram, "Perpetration of Violence"; Desmarais, Johnson, and Swartz, "Community Violence Perpetration and Victimization"; and Sadeh, Binder, and McNiel, "Recent Victimization Increases Risk for Violence."

8. This characterization is turned on its head in the character of Thomas Magnum in *Magnum, P.I.* (1980–88). Magnum's service is shown and discussed, but he is a rounded character who does not fall into the stereotype of the drunk, traumatized vet. This series was one of the first (indeed, to the best of my knowledge, the only) to provide this view of veterans in the person of the main character. Conversely, Principal Seymour Skinner in *The Simpsons* is a traumatized veteran, but his presentation is diametrically opposed to the others listed here. While Skinner does have moments of flashbacks and thousand-yard stares, he is neither violent nor alcoholic. Instead, he is meek to the point of childishness and is controlled by his mother, the setup for many jokes. His characterization is more "child-friendly," given that this is an all-ages television program, but when examined carefully, Skinner's traumatic presentation is equally disturbing.

9. See Shakespeare, *Henry IV, Part I*, act II, scene iii.

10. PTSD—post-traumatic stress disorder—is a profound and debilitating psychophysical response to a traumatic event. The individual will display a range of symptoms, including recurrent, involuntary, and intrusive distressing memories of the traumatic event; nightmares; flashbacks; hypervigilance; marked avoidance of external reminders that arouse distressing memories; and dissociation. See American Psychiatric Association, *Desk Reference to the Diagnostic Criteria from DSM-5*, 272–73. Not every individual will develop PTSD after a traumatic event; not every individual with PTSD will have the same symptoms and presentation. For more information, see Earle, *Comics, Trauma, and the New Art of War*; American Psychiatric Association, *Desk Reference to the Diagnostic Criteria from DSM-5*; Herman, *Trauma and Recovery*.

11. Wessely, "Life and Death of Private Harry Farr," 442.

12. The term "hysteria" finds its root in the Greek ὑστέρᾱ (*hustérā*, meaning "womb"). See Freud and Breuer, *Aetiology of Hysteria*.

13. I use both terms to show the demarcation between them. Trauma refers to the wider experience that is felt by many and can refer to a cultural lens through which these events are seen, as I demonstrate

toward the end of this chapter. PTSD refers to the specific medical diagnosis, which many veterans receive.

14. See American Psychiatric Association, *Diagnostic and Statistical Manual of Mental Disorders*, 3rd ed.
15. Earle, *Comics, Trauma, and the New Art of War*.
16. Westheider, *African American Experience in Vietnam*.
17. Earle, *Comics, Trauma, and the New Art of War*, 31. See also Freud and Breuer, *Aetiology of Hysteria*; Freud, *Beyond the Pleasure Principle*; Freud, *Moses and Monotheism*.
18. Whitehead, *Trauma Fiction*, 3.
19. Balaev, *Contemporary Approaches in Literary Trauma Theory*, 7.
20. In Freud's work on trauma, he uses the word *Nachträglichkeit* to describe the delayed onset of trauma after the individual has returned to "safety." See Freud and Breuer, *The Aetiology of Hysteria*; Freud, *Moses and Monotheism*.
21. Lomax, "Tradition."
22. Lomax, "To Face the Beast."
23. I use the term "failure" here to suggest that there is a lack in the U.S. military's response to their own people—there certainly *could* have been reintegration assistance and therapies offered to all returning service members—and to differentiate from the outright atrocities that were committed. There are several factors I could use to demonstrate this failure. For example, the statistics on homelessness among veterans suggest that not enough is being done to ensure that veterans are able to acquire both suitable housing and steady employment or, alternatively, adequate financial support. Current statistics are not consistent, but recent studies suggest that, on any given night, between forty thousand and seventy thousand veterans are unhoused (see Tsai and Rosenheck, "Risk Factors for Homelessness among US Veterans"; Tsai, Trevisan, et al., "Addressing Veteran Homelessness to Prevent Veteran Suicides"; Tsai, Pietrzak, and Szymkowiak, "Problem of Veteran Homelessness").
24. Earle, "'And Babies?'"
25. See Greenstein, "PTSD and Trauma."
26. Chute, "Secret Labor," 380.
27. American Psychiatric Association, *Desk Reference to the Diagnostic Criteria from DSM-5*, 272.
28. Delano and Ridgway, *Hellblazer*, 23.
29. He has taken lives in Vietnam, but this is the trauma and the war come home.

30. Delano and Ridgway, *Hellblazer*, 18.
31. Freud, *On the History of the Psycho-Analytic Movement Papers*, 244.
32. Freud, *On the History of the Psycho-Analytic Movement Papers*, 245.
33. Delano and Ridgway, *Hellblazer*, 23.
34. Delano and Ridgway, *Hellblazer*, 23.
35. Remarque, *All Quiet on the Western Front*.
36. "Re-upping" is the slang term for signing up for a further tour.
37. Coppola, *Apocalypse Now*.
38. Beatty et al., *DC Comics Encyclopedia*.
39. Ennis, Weston, et al., *Enemy Ace: War in Heaven*.
40. Earle, *Comics, Trauma, and the New Art of War*, 43.
41. American Psychiatric Association, *Desk Reference to the Diagnostic Criteria from DSM-5*, 272.
42. Pratt, *Enemy Ace*.
43. Pratt, *Enemy Ace*.
44. Caruth, *Unclaimed Experience*, 60.
45. Pratt, *Enemy Ace*.
46. Caruth, *Unclaimed Experience*, 60.
47. Pratt, *Enemy Ace*.
48. Neal, *National Trauma and Collective Memory*, 4.
49. Neal, *National Trauma and Collective Memory*, 4.
50. The Manson family murders are also referred to as the Tate-LaBianca murders. Across two nights in August 1969, seven people were murdered by members of a cultish group nicknamed the Family. Their names are Sharon Tate (whose unborn child, Paul, also died), Jay Sebring, Abigail Folger, Wojciech Frykowski, Steven Parent, Leon LaBianca, and Rosemary LaBianca.
51. Veitch, Irons, and Sheridan, *Legion of Charlies*.
52. Veitch, Irons, and Sheridan, *Legion of Charlies*.
53. Veitch, Irons, and Sheridan, *Legion of Charlies*.
54. Significant research has been undertaken into the high levels of addiction and death by suicide in returning veterans. See Pollock, Rhodes, and Boyle, "Estimating the Number of Suicides among Vietnam Veterans"; Stanton, "Drugs, Vietnam, and the Vietnam Veteran."
55. Fox, "Legion of Charlies."
56. Calley's defense at trial was that he was "following orders," sometimes named the "Nuremberg defense." This trial is one of a small number that led to the changing of regulations surrounding obedience to orders as a defense. In many penal codes, there is special

mention of situations in which a soldier may reject an order that "violates human dignity or if compliance would result in a criminal offense." This wording is taken from the Federal Republic of Germany's Wehrstrafgesetz (Military Penal Code), § 22 Verbindlichkeit des Befehls (Binding Nature of the Order, Error) ¶ 1 (March 30, 1957), https://www-gesetze--im--internet-de.translate.goog/wstrg/index.html?_x_tr_sl=de&_x_tr_tl=en&_x_tr_hl=en&_x_tr_pto=sc.
57. Fox, "Legion of Charlies."

CONCLUSION

1. "World Military Expenditure Reaches New Record High."
2. Mandelbaum, "Vietnam."
3. Postman, *Amusing Ourselves to Death*, 87.
4. Womack, *China and Vietnam*, 179.
5. Sarin and Dvoretsky, *Alien Wars*, 93–94.
6. Pribbenow, "Soviet-Vietnamese Intelligence Relationship."
7. Tran, *Vietnamerica*, 12.
8. Kaus, "View from the Vietnamese Diaspora," 5.
9. Hong, "Disorienting the Vietnam War," 15.
10. Kaus, "View from the Vietnamese Diaspora," 4.
11. Bui, *Best We Could Do*, 48.
12. Bui, *Best We Could Do*, 207.
13. Bui, *Best We Could Do*, 211.
14. Bui, *Best We Could Do*.
15. Bui, *Best We Could Do*, 216.
16. Bui, *Best We Could Do*, 185.
17. Tran, *Vietnamerica*, 108–9.
18. Kaus, "View from the Vietnamese Diaspora," 5.
19. Tran, *Vietnamerica*, 100, 236.
20. Said, "Homage to Joe Sacco," iii.
21. Nguyen, "Industries of Memory," 312.
22. Nguyen, "Industries of Memory," 312.

BIBLIOGRAPHY

Aaron, Jason, and Cameron Stewart. *The Other Side*. Portland: Image, 2017.

Acheson, Kris. "Silence in Dispute." *Annals of the International Communication Association* 31, no. 1 (2007): 2–59.

Ahrens, Courtney E. "Being Silenced: The Impact of Negative Social Reactions on the Disclosure of Rape." *American Journal of Community Psychology* 38, nos. 3-4 (2006): 263–74. https://doi.org/10.1007/s10464-006-9069-9.

Alighieri, Dante. *Inferno*. New York: Modern Library, 2002.

Altoff, Gerard T. *Oliver Hazard Perry and the Battle of Lake Erie*. Put-in-Bay OH: Perry, 1999.

American Psychiatric Association. *Desk Reference to the Diagnostic Criteria from DSM-5*. Washington DC: APA, 2013.

———. *The Diagnostic and Statistical Manual of Mental Disorders*. 3rd ed. Washington DC: APA, 1980.

Anderson, David. *The Columbia Guide to the Vietnam War*. New York: Columbia University Press, 2002.

Apple, R. "McNamara Recalls, and Regrets, Vietnam." *New York Times*, April 9, 1995.

Appy, Christian. *American Reckoning: The Vietnam War and Our National Identity*. New York: Viking, 2015.

Aristotle. *Politics*. Oxford: Oxford University, 1995.

Austin, Allan, and Patrick Hamilton. *All New, All Different? A History of Race and the American Superhero*. Austin: University of Texas, 2019.

Babiracki, Patryk. *Soviet Soft Power in Poland: Culture and the Making of Stalin's New Empire, 1943–1957*. Chapel Hill: University of North Carolina Press, 2015.

Backderf, Derf. "'My Claim to Fame Is Footnotes': An Interview with Derf Backderf." Interview by Vera Camden and Valentino Zullo. *Journal of Graphic Novels and Comics* 12, no. 4 (2020): 281–97.

"Back in the Real World." Doug Murray (writer), Wayne Vansant (penciller), Geof Isherwood (inker), and Phil Felix (colorist and letterer). *The 'Nam*, no. 41. New York: Marvel, 1990.

Balaban, John, trans. *Ca Dao Việt Nam: Vietnamese Folk Poetry*. Greensboro NC: Unicorn Press, 1980.

Balaev, Michelle. *Contemporary Approaches in Literary Trauma Theory*. London: Palgrave Macmillan, 2014.

Beard, David. "How Can You Not Shout, Now That the Whispering Is Done? Accounts of the Enemy in US, Hmong, and Vietnamese Soldiers' Literary Reflections on the War." *Humanities* 8, no. 4 (2019): 172.

Beattie, Keith. *The Scar That Binds: American Culture and the Vietnam War*. New York: New York University Press, 1998.

Beatty, Scott, Robert Greenburger, Phil Jiminez, and Dan Wallace. *The DC Comics Encyclopedia*. London: DK, 2008.

Benitez-Garcia, Gibran, Tomoaki Nakamura, and Masahide Kaneko. "Analysis of Differences between Western and East-Asian Faces Based on Facial Region Segmentation and PCA for Facial Expression Recognition." *AIP Conference Proceedings* 1807, no. 1 (2017): 1–10.

Berger, John. *Ways of Seeing*. London: Penguin, 1972.

Biguenet, John. *Silence*. London: Bloomsbury, 2015.

Bindeman, Steven. *Silence in Philosophy, Literature, and Art*. Leiden, Netherlands: Brill, 2017.

Bourdieu, Pierre. *Language and Symbolic Power*. Cambridge: Polity Press, 1992.

Brownmiller, Susan. *Against Our Will: Men, Women and Rape*. New York: Simon and Schuster, 1975.

Brox, Jane. *Silence: A Social History of One of the Least Understood Elements of Our Lives*. Boston: Houghton Mifflin Harcourt, 2019.

Bui, Thi. *The Best We Could Do*. New York: Abrams ComicArts, 2017.

Calverton, V. F. "The Cultural Barometer." *Current History* 45, no. 6 (1937): 101–6.

Caniff, Milton. "How to Spot a Jap." In *Pocket Guide to China*, 1st ed., by Special Service Division, Services of Supply, U.S. Army. Washington DC: U.S. Government Printing Office, 1942.

"Captured in Vietnam!" Stan Lee (writer), Gene Colan (penciller), Joe Sinnott (inker), and Sam Rosen (letterer). *Captain America*, no. 125. New York: Marvel, May 1970.

Caruth, Cathy. *Unclaimed Experience: Trauma, Narrative, and History*. Baltimore MD: Johns Hopkins University Press, 1996.

Cates, Donny, and Ryan Stegman. *Web of Venom: Ve'nam*. New York: Marvel, 2018.

Chireau, Yvonne. "White or Indian? Whiteness and Becoming the White Indian Comics Superhero." In *Unstable Masks: Whiteness and American Superhero Comics*, edited by Sean Guynes and Martin Lund, 193–211. Columbus: Ohio State University Press, 2020.

Choe, Jeanne Y., Linda A. Teplin, and Karen M. Abram. "Perpetration of Violence, Violent Victimization, and Severe Mental Illness: Balancing Public Health Concerns." *Psychiatric Services* 59, no. 2 (2008): 153–64.

Churchwell, Sarah. *The Many Lives of Marilyn Monroe*. London: Macmillan, 2005.

Chute, Hillary. "Secret Labor: Sketching the Connection between Poetry and Comics." *Poetry Magazine*, July/August 2013, 379–81.

Cohen, Richard. "From Saigon to Burke, There Is No Way Out." *Washington Post*, November 7, 1978.

"The Coming of the Yellow Claw!" Al Feldstein (writer), Joe Maneely (penciller and inker), and Stan Goldberg (colorist). New York: Marvel, 1956.

Cook, Bernard. *Women and War: A Historical Encyclopedia from Antiquity to the Present*. London: Bloomsbury, 2006.

Cooke, Jon, ed. *Comic Book Artist*, no. 4. Raleigh NC: Two Morrows, 1999.

Coppola, Francis Ford. *Apocalypse Now*. Beverly Hills CA: United Artists, 1979.

"Dangerous Assignment." Joe Gill (writer), Joe Sinnott (penciller), and Vince Collette (inker). *Sue and Sally Smith: Flying Nurses*, no. 48. Derby CT: Charlton Comics Group, November 1962.

Darwin, Charles. *The Expression of the Emotions in Man and Animal*. Oxford: Oxford University Press, 1872.

Davis, Nanette J. *Prostitution: An International Handbook on Trends, Problems, and Policies*. Westport CT: Greenwood Press, 1993.

Delano, Jamie, and John Ridgway. *Hellblazer*. Vol. 5. With Lovern Kindzierski (colorist), Todd Klein (letterer), and Dave McKean (cover artist) New York: DC Vertigo, 1988.

Desmarais, Sara, Kiersten Johnson, and Marvin Swartz. "Community Violence Perpetration and Victimization among Adults with Mental Illnesses." *American Journal of Public Health* 104, no. 12 (2014): 2342–49.

"Dien Bien Phu!" John Putnam (writer), John Severin (penciller and inker), Marie Severin (colorist), and Ben Oda (letterer). *Two-Fisted Tales*, no. 40. New York: EC Comics, December 1954–January 1955.

Di Paolo, Marc. *War, Politics and Superheroes: Ethics and Propaganda in Comics and Film*. Jefferson NC: McFarland, 2011.

Dittmar, Linda, and Gene Michaud, eds. *From Hanoi to Hollywood: The Vietnam War in American Film*. New Brunswick NJ: Rutgers University Press, 1991.

Dower, John. *War without Mercy: Race and Power in the Pacific War*. New York: Pantheon, 1986.

Dunne, Maryjane. "The Representation of Women in Comic Books, Post WWII through the Radical 60's." *McNair Scholars Online Journal* 2, no. 1 (2006): 81–91.

Earle, Harriet E. H. "'And Babies?' The Representation of Mỹ Lai in Vietnam War Comics." *Amerikastudien* (forthcoming).

———. *Comics, Trauma, and the New Art of War*. Jackson: University Press of Mississippi, 2017.

———. "Conflict Then; Trauma Now: Reading Vietnam across the Decades in American Comics." *European Journal of American Culture* 37, no. 2 (2018): 159–72.

———. "How Do Comics Engage with the Vietnam War? Two Photography Case Studies." *Americana: The Institute for the Study of American Popular Culture* 22, no. 2 (2023). https://americanpopularculture.com/journal/articles/fall_2023/earle.htm.

———. "A New Face for an Old Fight: Reimagining Vietnam in Vietnamese American Graphic Memoirs." *Studies in Comics* 9, no. 1 (June 2018): 87–105.

Eisner, Will. *Last Day in Vietnam: A Memory*. Milwaukie OR: Dark Horse Comics, 2013.

Elshtain, Jean. *Women and War*. Chicago: University of Chicago Press, 1995.

Ennis, Garth, and Goran Parlov. *Fury: My War Gone By*. With Dave Johnson (co-artist), Rob Steen (letterer), and Lee Loughridge (colorist). New York: Marvel, 2012.

———. *Punisher: The Platoon*. With Jordie Bellaire (co-artist and colorist) and Rob Steen (letterer). New York: Marvel, 2017.

Ennis, Garth, Chris Weston, Christian Alamy, and Russ Heath. *Enemy Ace: War in Heaven*. New York: DC, 2003.

Ennis, Garth, Darick Robertson, and Tom Palmer. *The Punisher: Born*. New York: Marvel, 2011.

Ennis, Garth, Jacen Burrows, and Goran Parlov. *Get Fury*. New York: Marvel, 2024.

Epstein, Daniel Robert. "Don Lomax's Vietnam Memories." Newsarama, August 28, 2003. Accessed July 21, 2022 (site discontinued). http://forum.newsarama.com/showthread.php?t=5378.

Epstein, Edward Jay. *Between Fact and Fiction*. New York: Vintage, 1975.

Ethnic Groups in Vietnam: An Analysis of Key Indicators from the 2009 Vietnam Census. Hanoi, Vietnam: United Nations Population Fund, 2011.

Fellman, Sandi. *The Japanese Tattoo*. New York: Abbeville, 1986.

Foucault, Michel. *The History of Sexuality: The Will to Knowledge*. London: Penguin, 2008

Fox, M. Steven. "The Legion of Charlies." Underground Comix Collection, 2013. https://comixjoint.com/legionofcharlies-1st.html.

Frank, Jerome, and Andrei Melville. "The Enemy Image and the Process of Change." In *Emerging New Thinking: Soviet and Western Scholars Issue a Challenge to Build a World Beyond War*, edited by Anatoly Gromyko and Martin Hellman, 198–207. New York: Walker, 1988.

Freud, Sigmund. *Beyond the Pleasure Principle*. In *The Standard Edition of the Complete Psychological Works of Sigmund Freud*, vol. 18, translated by James Strachey. London: Vintage, 2003.

———. *Moses and Monotheism*. In *The Standard Edition of the Complete Psychological Works of Sigmund Freud*, vol. 23, translated by James Strachey. London: Vintage, 2001.

———. *On the History of the Psycho-Analytic Movement Papers on Metapsychology and Other Works*. In *The Standard Edition of the Complete Psychological Works of Sigmund Freud*, vol. 2, translated by James Strachey. London: Vintage, 2001.

Freud, Sigmund, and Josef Breuer. *The Aetiology of Hysteria*. In *The Standard Edition of the Complete Psychological Works of Sigmund Freud*, vol. 2, translated by James Strachey. London: Vintage, 2001.

"Ghost Battalion." Joe Gill (writer), Charles Nicholas (penciller), and Vince Alascia (inker). *Army War Heroes*, no. 14. Derby CT: Charlton Comics Group, June 1966.

Gilkes, Madi. "Missing from History: The Other Prisoners of War.' *Trouble and Strife*, no. 41 (2000). https://www.troubleandstrife.org/articles/issue-41/missing-from-history-the-other-prisoners-of-war/.

"The Good Old Days." Doug Murray (writer), Michael Golden and Wayne Vansant (pencillers), Wayne Vansant and Geof Isherwood (inkers), Phil Felix (colorist), and Kurt Hathaway (letterer). *The 'Nam*, no. 7. New York: Marvel, June 1987.

Goodwin, Archie. *Blazing Combat*. With Frank Frazetta, Wallace Wood, John Severin, Alex Toth, Al Williamson, Russ Heath, Reed Crandall, Joe Orlando, and Gene Colon. Seattle: Fantagraphics, 2018.

Goscha, Christopher. *Vietnam: A New History*. New York: Basic Books, 2016.

Gould, Kenneth A. "The Ecological Costs of Militarization." *Peace Review: A Journal of Social Justice* 19, no. 3 (2007): 331–34.

Greenstein, Luna. "PTSD and Trauma: Not Just for Veterans." *National Alliance on Mental Illness* (blog), November 8, 2017. https://www.nami.org/active-duty/ptsd-and-trauma-not-just-for-veterans/.

Grell, Mike. "M.I.A." *Jon Sable, Freelance*, nos. 12–13. Evanston IL: First Comics, 1984.

Guillemot, François. "Death and Suffering at First Hand: Youth Shock Brigades during the Vietnam War (1950–1975)." *Journal of Vietnamese Studies* 4, no. 3 (October 2009): 17–60.

Gustafsson, Mai Lan. "'Freedom. Money. Fun. Love.': The Warlore of Vietnamese Bargirls." *Oral History Review* 38, no. 2 (2011): 308–30.

Hall, Nicholas. "The Wasp's Troublesome Children: Culture, Satire, and the Anti-Chinese Movement in the American West." *California History* 90, no. 2 (2013): 42–76.

"The Happy Hunting Ground." Joe Gill (writer) and Norman Nodel (penciller and inker). *Cheyenne Kid*, no. 58. Derby CT: Charlton Comics Group, October 1966.

Hayslip, Le Ly. *When Heaven and Earth Changed Places*. New York: Doubleday, 1989.

Hellmann, John. *American Myth and the Legacy of Vietnam*. New York: Columbia University Press, 1986.

Herman, Judith Lewis. *Trauma and Recovery: The Aftermath of Violence—From Domestic Abuse to Political Terror*. New York: Basic Books, 1992.

Hill, Joe. *The Cape 1969*. With Jason Ciaramella (coauthor) and Nelson Daniel (artist). San Diego: IDW, 2013.

Hirsch, Paul. *Pulp Empire: The Secret History of Comic Book Imperialism*. Chicago: University of Chicago Press, 2021.

———. "'This Is Our Enemy': The Writers' War Board and Representations of Race in Comic Books, 1942–1945." *Pacific Historical Review* 83, no. 3 (2014): 448–86.

Holmes, Richard. *The Oxford Companion to Military History*. Oxford: Oxford University Press, 2001.

Hong, Caroline. "Disorienting the Vietnam War: GB Tran's *Vietnamerica* as Transnational and Transhistorical Graphic Memoir." *Asian American Literature: Discourses and Pedagogies* 5 (2014): 11–22.

Hung, Mai Van, and Sunyoung Pak. "The Impact of Environment on Morphological and Physical Indexes of Vietnamese and South Korean Students." *VNU Journal of Science* 24 (2008): 50–55.

Huxley, David. "Naked Aggression: American Comic Books and the Vietnam War." In *Tell Me Lies about Vietnam: Cultural Battles for the Meaning of War*, edited by Alf Louvre and Jeffrey Walsh, 88–110. Milton Keynes, England: Open University Press, 1988.

———. "'The Real Thing': New Images of Vietnam in American Comic Books." In *Vietnam Images: War and Representation*, edited by Jeffrey Walsh and James Aulich, 160–70. Basingstoke, England: Macmillan, 1989.

"Indo-China Raid." Charles Nicholas (penciller) and Chuck Cuidera (inker). *G.I. Combat* 1, no. 15. New York: Quality Comics, June 1954.

"Iron Man Is Born!" Stan Lee and Larry Lieber (writers), Jack Kirby (artist), Don Heck (penciller and inker), Stan Goldberg (colorist), and Art Simek (letterer). *Tales of Suspense*, no. 39. New York: Marvel, March 1963.

Jahnke, R., and T. H. Jahnke. "The Politics of Māori Image and Design." *Pukenga Korero* 7, no. 1 (2003): 5–31.

James, David, and Rick Berg. "College Course File: Representing the Vietnam War." *Journal of Film and Video* 41, no. 4 (1989): 60–74.

Jeffords, Susan. *The Remasculinization of America: Gender and the Vietnam War*. Bloomington: Indiana University Press, 1989.

Kakihara, Kuniharu. "The Post-9/11 Paradigm Shift and Its Effects on East Asia." IIPS Policy Paper 292E, Institute for International Policy Studies, Tokyo, Japan, January 2003. https://npi.or.jp/en/research/data/bp292e.pdf.

Kaus, Alaina. "A View from the Vietnamese Diaspora: Memories of Warfare and Refuge in GB Tran's *Vietnamerica*." *Mosaic: An Interdisciplinary Critical Journal* 49, no. 4 (2016): 1–19.

Kleinman, Loren. "Silence Is the Language of Rape." *Ms.*, July 26, 2018. https://msmagazine.com/2018/07/26/silence-is-the-language-of-rape/.

Kodosky, Robert. "Holy Tet Westy! Graphic Novels and the Vietnam War." *Journal of Modern Culture* 44, no. 5 (2011): 1047–66.

Kubert, Joe, and Robert Kanigher. *Our Fighting Forces*, no. 100. New York: DC Comics, May 1966.

———. *Our Fighting Forces*, no. 105. New York: DC Comics, February 1967.
Kubrick, Stanley. *Full Metal Jacket*. Burbank CA: Warner Brothers, 1987.
Kurtzman, Harvey, and Harvey Gaines. *Two-Fisted Tales*. 24 issues. New York: EC Comics, November 1950–February 1955. Republished in *The Complete EC Library*. West Plains MO: Russ Cochran, 1980.
Landivar, Liana Christin. *Men in Nursing Occupations: American Community Survey Highlight Report*. Suitland MD: U.S. Government Census, 2013.
"Landscape." Archie Goodwin (writer), Joe Orlando (penciller and inker), and Ben Oda (letterer). *Blazing Combat*, no. 2. New York: Warren Magazine, January 1966.
Lawrence, Mark. *The Vietnam War: An International History in Documents*. Oxford: Oxford University Press, 2014.
Liew, Steven, Henry H. Chan, and John D. Rogers. "Consensus on Changing Trends, Attitudes, and Concepts of Asian Beauty." *Aesthetic Plastic Surgery* 40, no. 2 (April 2016): 193–201.
Lobe, Jim. "Three Major Networks Devoted a Full Five Minutes to Afghanistan in 2020." *Responsible Statecraft*, August 20, 2021. https://responsiblestatecraft.org/2021/08/20/three-major-networks-devoted-a-full-five-minutes-to-afghanistan-in-2020/.
Lomax, Don. "Birds of Prey." *Vietnam Journal*, no. 4. Bethel: Apple Comics, 1988.
———. "Cordon and Search." *Vietnam Journal*, no. 14. Bethel: Apple Comics, June 1990.
———. "Dustoff." *Vietnam Journal*, no. 7. Bethel: Apple Comics, 1988.
———. "To Face the Beast." *Vietnam Journal*, no. 8. Bethel: Apple Comics, 1989.
———. "Tradition." *Vietnam Journal*, no. 6. Bethel: Apple Comics, 1988.
Louvre, Alf, and Jeffrey Walsh, eds. *Tell Me Lies about Vietnam: Cultural Battles for the Meaning of War*. Milton Keynes, England: Open University Press, 1988.
Lund, Martin. "Rethinking the Jewish–Comics Connection." PhD diss., Lunds Universitet, 2013.
MacKinnon, Catherine A. *Feminism Unmodified: Discourses on Life and Law*. Cambridge MA: Harvard University Press, 1987.
MacLure, Maggie, Rachel Holmes, Liz Jones, and Christina MacRae. "Silence as Resistance to Analysis; or, On Not Opening One's Mouth Properly." *Qualitative Inquiry* 16, no. 6 (2010): 492–500.
Mandelbaum, Michael. "Vietnam: The Television War." *Daedalus* 111, no. 4 (1982): 157–69.

Manor, Ilan, and Guy Golan. "The Irrelevance of Soft Power." E-International Relations, October 19, 2020. https://www.e-ir.info/2020/10/19/the-irrelevance-of-soft-power/.

Marchetti, Gina. *Romance and the "Yellow Peril": Race, Sex, and Discursive Strategies in Hollywood Fiction*. Berkeley: University of California Press, 1993.

Marvel Preview, no. 2. With Ross Andru, Howard Chaykin, Gerry Conway, Tony DeZuniga, Mike Esposito, Frank Giacoia, Annette Kawecki, et al. New York: Magazine Management, July 1975.

"A Matter of Figures." Maurice Whitman (penciller) and Vince Colletta (inker). *Jungle War Stories*, no. 7. New York: Dell Comics, January 1964.

Melville, Herman. *Bartleby, the Scrivener: A Story of Wall-Street*. New York: Open Road Media, 2014.

Meyer Both College of Commercial Art. *Success in Commercial Art*. Chicago: Meyer Both College of Commercial Art, 1920.

Murray, Doug. "Interview with Brian Jacks." *Slush Factory*, May 14, 2009. https://web.archive.org/web/20160814080333/http://www.slushfactory.com/features/articles/052502-murray.php.

Murray, Doug, and Russ Heath. *Hearts and Minds: A Vietnam Love Story*. New York: Epic Comics, 1991.

Neal, Arthur. *National Trauma and Collective Memory: Extraordinary Events in the American Experience*. Armonk NY: Sharpe, 2005.

"The New Breed." Morris Waldinger (penciller) and Vince Alascia (inker). *War Heroes*, no. 23. Derby CT: Charlton Comics Group, March 1967.

"New Kind of War." Joe Gill (writer), Morris Waldinger (penciller), and Jon D'Agostino (inker). *Army War Heroes*, no. 13. Derby CT: Charlton Comics Group, March–April 1966.

Nguyen, Viet Thanh. "From Colonialism to Covid: Viet Thanh Nguyen on the Rise of Anti-Asian Violence." *Guardian*, April 3, 2021. https://www.theguardian.com/books/2021/apr/03/from-colonialism-to-covid-viet-thanh-nguyen-on-the-rise-of-anti-asian-violence.

———. "Industries of Memory: The Vietnam War in Art." In *American Studies as Transnational Practice: Turning toward the Transpacific*, edited by Yuan Shu and Donald Pease, 311–39. Hanover NH: Dartmouth College Press, 2015.

———. *Nothing Ever Dies: Vietnam and the Memory of War*. Cambridge: Harvard University Press, 2016.

Ninh, Bảo. *Thân Phân Của Tihn Yêu*. Hanoi, Vietnam: Nhà Xuat Bon Hoi Nha Von, 1991. Translated into English by Phan Thanh Hao and edited by Frank Palmos as *The Sorrow of War: A Novel of North Vietnam*. New York: Riverhead Books, 1993.

Ntagteverenis, Paschalis. "L'ennemi comme monstre." *Sociétés* 80, no. 2 (2003): 41–50.

Nye, Joseph. *Bound to Lead: The Changing Nature of American Power*. New York: Basic Books, 1990.

O'Brien, Tim. *The Things They Carried*. London: Flamingo, 1991.

Park, Jinim. *Narratives of the Vietnam War by Korean and American Writers*. New York: Peter Lang, 2007.

Pollock, D., Philip Rhodes, and C. A. Boyle. "Estimating the Number of Suicides among Vietnam Veterans." *American Journal of Psychiatry* 147, no. 6 (1990): 772–76.

Postman, Neil. *Amusing Ourselves to Death: Public Discourse in the Age of Show Business*. London: Penguin, 1985.

Pratt, George. *Enemy Ace: War Idyll*. New York: DC Comics, 1990.

Pribbenow, Merle. "The Soviet-Vietnamese Intelligence Relationship during the Vietnam War: Cooperation and Conflict." Cold War International History Project Working Paper Series 73, Washington DC, Woodrow Wilson International Center for Scholars, December 11, 2014. https://www.wilsoncenter.org/sites/default/files/media/documents/publication/CWIHP_Working_Paper_73_Soviet-Vietnamese_Intelligence_Relationship_Vietnam_War.pdf.

Punisher Invades The 'Nam, nos. 52–53. Roger Salick (writer), Mike Harris (artist), and Ed Lazellari (colorist). New York: Marvel, 1991.

Punisher Invades The 'Nam, nos. 67–69. Chuck Dixon (writer), Kevin Kobasic (artist), and Phil Felix (colorist). New York: Marvel, 1992.

Race, Jeffrey. *War Comes to Long An: Revolutionary Conflict in a Vietnamese Province*. Berkeley: University of California Press, 1972.

"The Raiders' Roost." A. Albert (penciller and inker), Maurice Whitman, and John Belcastro. *Wings Comics*, no. 120. New York: Fiction House, 1953.

Randal, Jonathan. "Nhatrang Fights Vice 'Grottoes': Resort, Favored by Troopers, Is Scene of 350 Arrests." *New York Times*, April 28, 1967.

Reitberger, Reinhold, and Wolfgang J. Fuchs. *Comics: Anatomy of a Mass Medium*. London: Studio Vista, 1972.

Remarque, Erich Maria. *All Quiet on the Western Front*. London: Penguin, 2010.

"Requiem for a Red." Bill Fraccio (penciller) and Tony Tallarico (inker). *Jungle War Stories*, no. 1. New York: Dell Publishing, July–September 1962.

Richards, Dave. "Descent into Hell: Aaron Talks 'The Other Side.'" Comic Book Resources, February 24, 2006. https://www.cbr.com/descent-into-hell-aaron-talks-the-other-side/.

Rifas, Leonard. "Cold War Comics." *International Journal of Comic Art* 2, no 1 (2000): 3–32.

———. *Korean War Comic Books*. Durham NC: McFarland, 2021.

———. "Korean War Comic Books and the Militarization of US Masculinity." *positions: asia critique* 23, no. 4 (2015): 618–31.

———. "Mecanismos de censura de comic books en Estados Unidos durante la Guerra de Corea (con el Dr. Fredric Wertham)." *Tebeosfera* 21 (2022). https://www.tebeosfera.com/documentos/mecanismos_de_censura_de_comic_books_en_estados_unidos_durante_la_guerra_de_corea_con_el_dr._fredric_wertham.html.

Sadeh, Naomi, Renée L. Binder, and Dale E. McNiel. "Recent Victimization Increases Risk for Violence in Justice-Involved Persons with Mental Illness." *Law and Human Behavior* 38, no. 2 (2014): 119–25.

Said, Edward. "Homage to Joe Sacco." Introduction to *Palestine*, by Joe Sacco. Seattle WA: Fantagraphics Books, 2001.

Salaita, Steven. "Beyond Orientalism and Islamophobia: 9/11, Anti-Arab Racism, and the Mythos of National Pride." CR: *The New Centennial Review* 6, no. 2 (2006): 245–66.

Sarin, Oleg, and Lev Dvoretsky. *Alien Wars: The Soviet Union's Aggressions against the World, 1919 to 1989*. New York City: Presidio Press, 1996.

Senate Committee on the Judiciary, Comic Books and Juvenile Delinquency. *Code of the Comics Magazine Association of America, Inc.* Washington DC: U.S. Government Printing Office, October 26, 1954.

Seymour, Margaret. "The Problem with Soft Power." Foreign Policy Research Institute, September 14, 2020. https://www.fpri.org/article/2020/09/the-problem-with-soft-power/.

Shakespeare, William. *Henry IV, Part I*. Oxford: Oxford University Press. 2008.

Sheehi, Stephen. *Islamophobia: The Ideological Campaign against Muslims*. Atlanta GA: Clarity Press, 2011.

Slotkin, Richard. *Regeneration through Violence: The Mythology of the American Frontier, 1600–1860*. Norman: University of Oklahoma Press, 1973.

Smith, Zoe D. "4 Colorism, or, The Ashiness of It All." *Women Write about Comics* (blog) May 24, 2019. https://womenwriteaboutcomics.com/2019/05/4-colorism-or-the-ashiness-of-it-all/.

Solomon, Norman. *War Made Invisible: How America Hides the Human Toll of Its Military Machine*. New York: New Press, 2023.

"Somebody Turn Him Off!" Joe Gill (writer), Sam Glanzman (artist), Charlotte Jetter (letterer), and Sal Gentile (editor). *Fightin' Marines*, no. 95. Derby CT: Charlton Comics Group, January 1971.

Soper, Kerry D. *We Go Pogo: Walt Kelly, Politics, and American Satire*. Jackson: University Press of Mississippi, 2012.

Spiegelman, Art. *MetaMaus: A Look Inside a Modern Classic, Maus*. New York: Pantheon Books, 2011.

Spivak, Gayatri. "Can the Subaltern Speak?" In *Marxism and the Interpretation of Culture*, edited by Cary Nelson and Lawrence Grossberg, 271–313. Basingstoke, England: Macmillan, 1988.

Stanton, Duncan. "Drugs, Vietnam, and the Vietnam Veteran." *American Journal of Drug and Alcohol Abuse* 3, no. 4 (1976): 557–70.

"Star-Studded Blockbuster." Charles Nicholas (penciller) and Vince Colletta (inker). *Jungle War Stories*, no. 8. New York: Dell Comics, April 1964.

Staszak, Jean-François. "Other/Otherness." In *International Encyclopedia of Human Geography*, 8th ed., edited by Rob Kitchin and Nigel Thrift. Amsterdam: Elsevier, 2008.

Stein, Murray, and Barbara Rothbaum. "175 Years of Progress in PTSD Therapeutics: Learning from the Past." *American Journal of Psychiatry* 175, no. 6 (2018): 508–16.

Stur, Heather. *Beyond Combat: Women and Gender in the Vietnam War Era*. Cambridge: Cambridge University Press, 2011.

Su, Phung. "Women of the Vietnam War: Fighting for the Revolution." Master's thesis, California State University, Fullerton, 2013. ProQuest (1523873).

Super Green Beret, no. 1. With Carl Pfeufer, William J. Dolan, Otto Binder, Wayne Marston, and Ben Oda. New York: Lightning Comics, April 1967.

Taylor, Keith Weller. *The Birth of Vietnam*. Berkeley: University of California Press, 1983.

Taylor, Sandra C. *Vietnamese Women at War: Fighting for Ho Chi Minh and the Revolution*. Lawrence: University Press of Kansas, 1999.

Thai, Hung Cam. *Insufficient Funds: The Culture of Money in Low-Wage Transnational Families*. Stanford: Stanford University Press, 2014.

Thomas, Terry, Han Kang, and Nancy Dalager. "Mortality among Women Vietnam Veterans, 1973–1987." *American Journal of Epidemiology* 134, no. 9 (1991): 973–80.

"Three Day Pass." Doug Murray (writer), Michael Golden (penciller), Armando Gil (inker), and Phil Felix (colorist and letterer). *The 'Nam*, no. 3. New York: Marvel, February 1987.

Tran, GB. *Vietnamerica*. New York: Villard, 2010.

Tsai, Jack, and Robert Rosenheck. "Risk Factors for Homelessness among US Veterans." *Epidemiologic Reviews* 37, no. 1 (2015): 177–95.

Tsai, Jack, Louis Trevisan, Minda Huang, and Robert Pietrzak. "Addressing Veteran Homelessness to Prevent Veteran Suicides." *Psychiatric Services* 69, no. 8 (2018): 935–37.

Tsai, Jack, Robert Pietrzak, and Dorota Szymkowiak. "The Problem of Veteran Homelessness: An Update for the New Decade." *American Journal of Preventive Medicine* 60, no. 6 (2021): 774–80.

Turley, William. "Women in the Communist Revolution in Vietnam." *Asian Survey* 12, no. 9 (1972): 793–805.

Turner-Gottschang, Karen, and Thanh Hao Phan. *Even the Women Must Fight: Memories of War from North Vietnam*. Hoboken NJ: Wiley, 1999.

Turse, Nick. *Kill Anything That Moves: The Real American War in Vietnam*. New York: Henry Holt, 2013.

United Nations. *The World's Women, 1970–1990: Trends and Statistics*. ST/ESA/STAT/SER K/8. New York: United Nations, 1991. https://unstats.un.org/unsd/demographic-social/products/worldswomen/documents/ww1990.pdf.

Veitch, Tom, Greg Irons, and Dave Sheridan. *The Legion of Charlies*. San Francisco: Last Gasp Eco-Funnies, 1971.

Vonnegut, Kurt. *Slaughterhouse-Five*. London: Vintage, 1991.

Vuic, Kara Dixon. *Officer, Nurse, Woman: The Army Nurse Corps in the Vietnam War*. Baltimore MD: Johns Hopkins University Press, 2010.

Vuorinen, Marja. *Enemy Images in War Propaganda*. Newcastle upon Tyne, England: Cambridge Scholars, 2012.

Wagner, Geoffrey. "Parade of Pleasure: A Study of Popular Iconography in the U.S.A." *Journal of Aesthetics and Art Criticism* 14, no. 3 (1956): 398–400.

Wagner, Roi. "Silence as Resistance before the Subject, or Could the Subaltern Remain Silent?" *Theory, Culture, and Society* 29, no. 6 (2012): 99–124.

"A Walk in the Sun." Carl Memling (writer), Maurice Whitman (penciller), and Vince Colletta (inker). *Jungle War Stories*, no 2. New York: Dell Publishing, January–March 1963.

Walsh, Jeffrey, and James Aulich. *Vietnam Images: War and Representation*. Basingstoke, England: Macmillan, 1989.

Weaver, Gina Marie. *Ideologies of Forgetting: Rape in the Vietnam War*. Albany: State University of New York Press, 2010.

Wessely, Simon. "The Life and Death of Private Harry Farr." *Journal of the Royal Society of Medicine* 99 (2006): 440–43.

Westheider, James. *The African American Experience in Vietnam: Brothers in Arms*. Lanham MD: Rowman and Littlefield, 2008.

Whitehead, Anne. *Trauma Fiction*. Edinburgh, Scotland: Edinburgh University Press, 2004.

Whitlock, Gillian. "Autographics: The Seeing 'I' of Comics." *Modern Fiction Studies* 52, no. 4 (2006): 965–79.

Winter, Jay. *War beyond Words*. Cambridge: Cambridge University Press, 2017.

Womack, Brantly. *China and Vietnam*. Cambridge: Cambridge University Press, 2006.

"World Military Expenditure Reaches New Record High." Stockholm International Peace Research Institute, April 24, 2023. https://www.sipri.org/media/press-release/2023/world-military-expenditure-reaches-new-record-high-european-spending-surges.

Wright, Bradford. *Comic Book Nation: The Transformation of Youth Culture in America*. Baltimore MD: John Hopkins University Press, 2001.

Xing, Jun. *Asian America through the Lens: History, Representations, and Identity*. Lanham MD: Rowman Altamira, 1988.

Young, Richard. "There Is Nothing Grittier Than a 'Grunt's Eye View': American Comic Books and the Popular Memory of the Vietnam War." *Australasian Journal of American Studies* 34, no. 2 (2015): 75–93.

Zdarsky, Chip, Mark Bagley, Andrew Hennessy, and Frank D'Armata. "The '70s." *Spider-Man: Life Story*, no. 2. New York: Marvel, 2019.

Zdarsky, Chip, Mark Bagley, John Dell, and Frank D'Armata. "The '60s." *Spider-Man: Life Story*, no. 1. New York: Marvel, 2019.

Zweig, Stefan. *The World of Yesterday*. London: Pushkin Press, 2009.

INDEX

Page numbers in italics refer to illustrations.

Aaron, Jason, 68, 94
Adams, Eddie, 61, 155
Afghanistan, 62
Agnew, Spiro, 126
All Quiet on the Western Front (film), 119
Apocalypse Now (film), 119, 147n83
Appy, Christian, 105
Aristotle, 102–3
Army War Heros (comic), 12

Backderf, Derf, 19
Balabar, John, 131
Battle of Điện Biên Phủ, 42–45
Battle of Lake Erie, 29
The Best We Could Do (comic), 20, 132–35
The Big Lebowski (film), 104
Blazing Combat (comic), 12
Bourdieu, Pierre, 141n4
Breaking Bad (TV show), 104
Breuer, Josef, 106–8
Brownmiller, Susan, 76, 81
Bui, Th., 20, 132–38

Calley, William, 112, 125–26
Calverton, V. F., 2
Cambodia, 25, 78, 147n83
Cannif, Milton, 37
The Cape (comic), 66

The Cape 1969 (comic), 66–67, *67*
Captain America (comic), 48
Castro, Fidel, 42
Cheyenne Kid (comic), 35, 48–49
China, 32–33, 93, 130
Cinder and Ashe (comic), 55
comics: autographic, 18–19; censorship of, 6–7, 13–16, 88–89, 142n12; color use in, 48–54, 65, 69, 88, 120–21; and Comic Magazine Association of America, 142n12, 149n50; encapsulation in, xii; nudity in, 90–92; printing of, 53; sexual violence in, 64, 76–85, *82*; soft power of, 5; superhero, 17–18, 63, 142n12
Communism, 5–8, 10
Cuba, 18

DC, 54, 68
de Gaulle, Charles, 21
Dell and Charlton, 9–13
Diagnostic and Statistical Manual of Mental Disorders (DSM), 106, 116, 151n10
Diệm, Ngô Đình, 10
Dong Xoai, Vietnam 1965 (comic), 18
Dower, John, 36

169

Eisner, Will, 18–19
Enemy Ace: War Idyll (comic), 105, 119–23
Ennis, Garth, 66

Fightin' Five (comic), 48
Fightin' Marines (comic), 13, 48
Forrest Gump (film), 104
Foucault, Michel, 20–21. *See also* silence
Freud, Sigmund, 106–7, 113, 117, 122, 152n20
Full Metal Jacket (film), 71, 88, 147n83
Fu Manchu, 33, 48, 100
Fury: My War Gone By (comic), 18, 63

Germany, 37
Giáp, Võ Nguyên, 43, 95–97
GI Joe (comic), 55
The Green Berets (film), 14, 54
Guerillas (comic), 66
Gulf Wars, 23

Hasford, Gustav, 68, 147n83
Hearts and Minds: A Vietnam Love Story (comic), 89–92
Heinemann, Larry, 77–78
Hellblazer (comic), 40, 55, 105, 113–19, 123, 126
Hollywood, 5, 15
The Human Fly (comic), 55

In-Country Nam (comic), 55, 143n34
Indochina. *See* Vietnam
International Geneva Conference, 8
Iraq, 62. *See also* Gulf Wars
Irons, Greg, 125–27
Islam. *See* Muslims

Japan, 33–37, 56
Jeffords, Susan, 74–75
John Sable, Freelance (comic), 59–61
Johnson, Lyndon B., 10
Jungle War Stories (comic), 9–10, 36, 45–47, 54, 59

Kanigher, Robert, 120
Kelly, Walt, 29
Kennedy, John F., 10
Kent State: Four Dead in Ohio (comic), 19
Kirby, Jack, 145n53
Korean War, 6–7, 10, 42
Kubert, Joe, 18–19, 120
Kurtzman, Harvey, 43
Kỳ, Nguyễn Cao, 146n76

Laos, 8, 25
Last Day in Vietnam: A Memory (comic), 18
Ledwell, Ronald, 143n34
The Legion of Charlies (comic), 105, 109, 123–26
Lém, Nguyễn Văn, 61
Lewis, Tom, 143n34
Lightning Comics, 50
Loan, Nguyễn Ngọc, 61, 135
Lomax, Don, 15, 88

Magnum, P.I. (TV show), 151n8
Malaysia, 134
Manson family murders, 125–26
Mao Zedong, 33
Marvel, 54, 150n69
Marvel Team-Up (comic), 55
McNamara, Robert, 1–2
Melville, Herman, 21
Miller, Jeffrey, 19
Minh, Dương Văn, 1

Minh, Ho Chi ("Uncle Ho"), 17, 48, 92, 129
Murray, Doug, 16, 56
Muslims, 4, 62
My Secret Life (comic), 99

The 'Nam (comic), 15–18, 55–59, 58, 63, 87, 101, 109–11
National Liberation Front (NLF, Viet Cong): defection from, 56; development of, 13, 135; elusiveness of, 45, 135; female combatants in, 74, 80–85, 95; flag of, 1; portrayal of, 36, 41–42, 45–52, 56–57, 64–66, 80–85; success of, 1, 10, 46, 89, 131; tunnels of, 12, 42, 93, 109, 122
Nguyen, Viet Thanh, 14–15, 20, 72, 137
9/11, 61–62, 124. *See also* War on Terror
Ninh, Bảo, 131
Nixon, Richard, 126
North Vietnam: and Ho Chi Minh Trail, 74; jungle associated with, 45–47; and People's Army of Vietnam, 1, 50–52, 65, 68–69, 74, 94; Soviet support of, 46, 130; territory of, 9; and Tet Offensive, 13, 61, 134
Nye, Joseph. *See* soft power

Orientalism, 32. *See also* Vietnamese people, portrayal of
The Other Side (comic), 68–70, 94–95
Our Army at War (comic), 120
Our Fighting Forces (comic), 50–53, 87

Paris Peace Accords, 14
Philippines, 37, 133

prisoners of war (POWs), 7, 59, 102
PS: The Preventive Maintenance Monthly (magazine), 19
PTSD (post-traumatic stress disorder), 27, 43, 64, 78, 83, 87, 99, 102–27, 151n8
publishers: DC, 54, 68; Dell and Charlton, 9–13; Lightning Comics, 50; Marvel, 54, 150n69; Survival Art Press, 143n34
The Punisher (comic), 18
The Punisher: Born (comic), 18, 64–66, 81, 82
The Punisher: The Platoon (comic), 18, 64–65, 83–85, 84, 95–97

Reagan, Ronald, 59
Rifas, Leonard, 6
Rohmer, Sax. *See* Fu Manchu
Roma people, 24
"Rusty Kali." *See* Calley, William

Said, Edward, 32, 137
Scalped (comic), 66
Scout (comic), 55
Seymour, Margaret, 4
Sgt. Fury and His Howling Commandoes (comic), 18
Sgt. Rock (comic), 55
Sheridan, David, 125–27
silence: as discourse, 3, 130; via omission, 31, 34, 55, 68, 78–79, 94, 99, 109; via racist portrayals, 31, 40–41, 59; and self-silencing, 21; via sexual violence, 66, 69, 75–85, 82, 107–9, 112, 125; and "unspeakability" of trauma, 27, 107–8; as violence, 5–6, 20–22, 75, 84. *See also* Vietnamese people, portrayal of

The Simpsons (TV show), 151n8
Sinti people, 24
soft power, 4–5
South Vietnam: and Army of the Republic of Vietnam, 10–11, 31, 45–47, 52, 80; territory of, 9; U.S. support for, 8–10, 31, 46; village associated with, 45; and Women's Armed Forces Corp, 74
Soviet Union, 4, 46, 130
Stewart, Cameron, 68, 94
Stranger Things (TV show), 104
Strange Tales (comic), 18
Sue and Sally Smith: Flying Nurses (comic), 99–101
Super Green Beret (comic), 50, *51*, 53
Survival Art Press, 143n34

Tales of Suspense (comic), 48
Taxi Driver (film), 104
Tempus Fugitive (comic), 55
Tran, GB, 20, 132–38
Truman, Harry, 6
Trưng, Nhị, 93–94
Trưng, Trắc, 93–94
Two-Fisted Tales (comic), 42–43

United States: and "Americanization" of Vietnam War, 11; Asian immigrants to, 32–38, 52, 133; and Central Intelligence Agency, 18, 63; and Chinese Exclusion Act, 32; colonial rule of Philippines by, 37, 133; and Indigenous Americans, 49; and Writers' War Board, 37
U.S. military: and Department of Defense, 6; and Executive Order 9981, 50; failure of, to protect veterans, 111; Indigenous American soldiers in, 49–50, 54; and Military Assistance Advisory Group, 6, 45–47; "noble cause" rhetoric of, 59; nurses in, 98–101, 107; and Purple Heart, 14; and PX (Post Exchange), 12, 88, 149n47; racial integration of, 107; racial segregation in, 50; size and spending of, 129; tanks of, 8; whiteness of, *51*, 52; and Winter Soldier Investigation, 77; and Women's Armed Services Integration Act, 73; and Women's Army Corp, 73. *See also* veterans, portrayal of

van Es, Hubert, 136
Vechhio, Mary Ann, 19
Veitch, Tom, 125–27
veterans, portrayal of: as addicted, 103, 111, 115–17, 126, 151n8, 153n54; as cannibals, 125–26; as "crazy," 27, 103–5, 110, 115–18; as domestic abusers, 116–18; as "heroic," 7, 17, 44, 78; as hypervigilant, 114–15, 151n10; as "hysterical," 107; as insomniacs, 114; as isolated, 119, 123, 126, 151n10; as masculine, 5, 44, 85, 103, 130; as mourning and grieving, 117–19; with nightmares and flashbacks, 105, 110, 114–16, 151n8, 151n10; as suicidal, 153n54; as traumatized, 27, 43, 64, 78, 83, 87, 99, 102–27, 151n8; as violent, 103–4, 116, 150n7; as white, 104–7, 130; as working-class, 107, 121
Viet Cong. *See* National Liberation Front (NLF, Viet Cong)

Vietnam: Chinese war against, 93–94; and Communist Party, 135; and Da Nang, 44; and Điện Biên Phủ, 8; division of, 8, 46; ethnic groups in, 40; French colonial rule of, 8–10, 42–43, 56, 90–91, 132–35; and Hồng Bàng dynasty, 40; independence of, 8; Japanese invasion of, 56; languages in, 40, 131; and National Police, 74; and Radio Saigon, 1; and Saigon, 1–2, 14, 86–87, 134–36. *See also* North Vietnam; South Vietnam; Vietnam War

Vietnamerica: A Family's Journey (comic), 20, 132–35

Vietnamese military: Army of the Republic of Vietnam, 10–11, 31, 45–47, 52, 80; People's Army of Vietnam, 1, 50–52, 65, 68–69, 74, 94; People's Self-Defense Forces, 74; Việt Minh, 7–8, 42, 56, 135. *See also* National Liberation Front (NLF, Viet Cong)

Vietnamese people, portrayal of: as absent, 31, 34, 40–45, 55, 59, 63, 138; as animalistic, 31–33, 40, 51, 52, 57, 66; as cowardly, 10, 42, 46, 96, 136; as "the enemy," 25–26, 30–31, 35, 38–41, 46, 68, 74; as infantile, 9, 46–47; as lazy, 47; as "mixed race," 90; with pidgin English, 48; with tattoos, 66–68, 67; with visual racism, 26, 30, 34–37, 48–52, 51, 57, 66, 88; as weak, 36, 51, 60

Vietnam Journal (comic), 15, 55, 79–80, 88, 101, 109–11

Vietnam War: "Americanization" of, 11; and Battle of Hue, 90–91; chemical warfare in, 29; end of, 14, 136; guerrilla warfare in, 42, 49, 129; measures of success of, 1–2; and "mere gook rule," 39–40; and Mỹ Lai massacre, 77, 112, 125; mythogenesis of, 5, 24, 41, 130–32, 138; naming of, 25; "newness" of, 11–12; outbreak of, as unclear, 6, 44, 141n1; protests against, 11, 19; as "televised" war, 11, 14, 22, 129; U.S. failure to achieve victory in, 1–2, 47, 138

violence, symbolic, 141n4

Vonnegut, Kurt, 102

von Richthofen, Manfred ("Red Baron"), 120

Vuorinen, Maria, 38–39

War Heroes (comic), 12, 48

War on Terror, xi, 23, 62. *See also* 9/11

Warren, James, 12

Wasp (comic), 32–33

Web of Venom: Ve'Nam (comic), 63

Wertham, Fredric, 142n12

Westmoreland, William, 13

Wings Comics (comic), 7

women and girls: as bar girls, 86–87, 136; as caregivers, 26, 46, 72, 94, 98; clothes of, 87–88, 91, 95, 100, 146n60; as combatants, 64–65, 71–74, 80–85, 92–97; commodification of, 72, 85–92; femininity of, 26; labor erasure of, 3, 23, 73–74, 97–99; as nurses, 98–101, 107; sexual violence committed against, 66, 69, 75–85, 82, 107–9, 112, 125; as sex workers, 71–73, 85–92, 125, 135, 149n47; as snipers, 150n68;

women and girls (*cont*)
    and U.S. womanhood, 72, 98–100; white men's supposed preference for, 92

World War I, 105-6, 120

World War II: and change in attitudes toward Japan, 33–35, 38, 42, 45; comics about, 7, 24, 44, 145n36, 149n44; and the Holocaust, 24, 120; novels about, 102; and Pearl Harbor attack, xi, 45

Yellow Claw (comic), 38

In the Encapsulations: Critical Comics Studies series

Storytelling in "Kabuki": An Exploration of Spatial Poetics of Comics
Steen Ledet Christiansen

Silence in the Quagmire: The Vietnam War in U.S. Comics
Harriet E. H. Earle

The New Nancy: Flexible and Relatable Daily Comics in the Twenty-First Century
Jeff Karnicky

Aquaman and the War against Oceans: Comics Activism and Allegory in the Anthropocene
Ryan Poll

To order or obtain more information on these or other University of Nebraska Press titles, visit nebraskapress.unl.edu.

www.ingramcontent.com/pod-product-compliance
Lightning Source LLC
Chambersburg PA
CBHW030236240426
43663CB00037B/1166